The Fine Structure Constant

For
Laurey and Richard Fisher
with every good wish.

Keith Whittaker

Quaerendo invenietis!

Porcupine Lodge
February 25, 2001

The Fine Structure Constant

Cumulo-Contextual
Lexico-Heuristic Verse

Philosophical Explorations
via
A Poetics of Consciousness

Keith Whittingslow

Writer's Showcase
San Jose New York Lincoln Shanghai

The Fine Structure Constant

Cumulo-Contextual
Lexico-Heuristic Verse

Philosophical Explorations
via
A Poetics of Consciousness

All Rights Reserved © 2000 by Keith Whittingslow

No part of this book may be reproduced or transmitted in any form or by any means, graphic, electronic, or mechanical, including photocopying, recording, taping, or by any information storage or retrieval system, without the permission in writing from the publisher.

Writer's Showcase
an imprint of iUniverse.com, Inc.

For information address:
iUniverse.com, Inc.
5220 S 16th, Ste. 200
Lincoln, NE 68512
www.iuniverse.com

ISBN: 0-595-09831-2

Printed in the United States of America

Dedication

This volume is dedicated to the omni-polar *sprachgeistian* reflections eternally recurrent in the musings of Urizen, Dionysus, Zarathustra and . . . the *other*.

> There is an undoubted affinity between the philosopher and the poet: both take as their point of departure the ultimate equation of being and nothing.
>
> The operative mode of poetic thought is imagining, and imagination consists, essentially, of the ability to place contrary or divergent realities in relationship.
>
> Each poem, whatever its subject or form and the ideas that shape it, is first and foremost a miniature animated cosmos. The poem unites the 'ten thousand things' that make up the universe.
>
> Octavio Paz
The Other Voice

The Fine Structure Constant

> And how could I endure to be a man, if man were not also poet and reader of riddles and . . . a way to new dawns.
>
> Friedrich Nietzsche
> *Thus Spoke Zarathustra*

Contents

FOREWARD XI
PREFACE XIII

I. Speculative-Heuristic Verse 1

Words as Dimensional Transforms 3
Subjectionality..5
Life, Energy, Wisdom and Cosmos 7
Re-Cognizing and re-Membering 8
A Socratic Koan..10
Sourceology 11
The Fine Structure Constant 13
The Core 20
Celestial Resonance 22
The Wind at Djemila: Remembering Camus 24
Exoteric/Esoteric 26
Winter Solstice...31
Snarl 33
Quantum Etheric Cosmology 34
The Whole Enchilada 36
O Felix Culpa...38
Grin 40
The Evolution of Consciousness 41
The Trap...43
Icebergs in Outer Space 45
Transparencies...47
Some Names, Attributes, and/or Characteristics of the Numinous....50
The Dream..52

The Fine Structure Constant

Summer Solstice 58
Molte Colore 60
Lucid Breathing 63
The Stoker 65
Process, Truth, and Provisionality 67
The Double-Truth Universe 69
The Edge 71
Toccata Gnostica Semantica 74
A Meditation 76
Japhy Rider 81
Air Fare 85
The Home Office...87
Cascade 89
Gliding...91
Prism 94
Progressions..97
Vak 98
Journeying...101
Essence and Substance 104
Driven 107
Passages 109
Openings and Transitions...111
Relation and Reciprocity 113
Dasein and Ayin 115
Nexus 119
The Perfume River 123
Abeam of Reality...126
Some Aspects of Circularity and Wholeness...................................129
Golden Elixir 135
Twilight 140
Suspense..142
Methodology 145

Zeal	147
Soul's Locus	149
Subsets	151
II. Jnanaic Senryu (Series)	153
III. Birthday Poems	169
L	171
Ephemeral Joy	173
North Coast Canticle	175
Projective (Revolutionary) Dimensions of Barbara Carlson's Art on Her Birthday	177
IV. The Search For Meaning	179
Points of View	181
From Food-Chain to Mind-Link	183
The Interface	187
Origin	189
Meaning	191
Tears	193
Trace and Texture	195
Precision	197
Analogues	199
Eidos	201
Tension	203
Means to Truth	205
Art and Science	207
Mnemonics	209
Still Life	211
Primals	213

The Fine Structure Constant

Eiron	215
Syzygy	219
Synchronicity	221
Seance	223
Evolutes and Hermeneuts	225
Chalcedony	228
Spinal Tap	231
Helix	234
Mica and the Pure Look	236
Mind Sutra	238
Logoic Enigmata	241
Interlude	243
Vectors	245
Steady State	247
Trope/*h*	250
ABOUT THE AUTHOR	253

Foreword

$$\alpha = \frac{e^2}{hc}$$

The square of the unit electrical charge (the charge of the electron) divided by the product of the velocity of light multiplied by Planck's constant — is referred to as the *fine structure constant.*

> **The New Physics**
> Paul Davies Ed., Cambridge, NY, 1991
>
> **The Becoming of Time**
> Lawrence W. Fagg, Scholars Press, Atlanta, 1995

The *nuclear particles*, electron and proton, **created by photons,** are the first occurrence of permanent mass and charge, the basic substance of the universe, **as compared with the activity of the** *light that created them*. But not all of this activity (or, more correctly, angular momentum) is condensed into mass. For reasons which are still unknown, **1/137** of the angular momentum **remains uncommitted, and free.** (This **1/137**

The Fine Structure Constant

is known as the *fine structure constant*.) It is this "freedom" which manifests itself in the uncertainty of position and momentum that characterizes the fundamental particles.

Angular momentum, quantum of action, and Planck's constant are synonymous. Also synonymous, is **light**; in fact *light = quanta of action = wholes = first cause.*

That the electron "possesses" an innate uncertainty is implicit from the definition of the *fine structure constant.* See also Northrop's introduction to Heisenberg, wherein Northrop emphasizes that the uncertainty of the electron is *ontological,* not just epistemological. Heisenberg, W. *Physics and Philosophy.* New York: Harper and Row, 1958.

Light, itself without mass, can create protons and electrons which have mass. Light has no charge, yet the particles it creates do. Since light is without mass, it is **non-physical**, of a different nature than physical particles. In fact, for the **photon**, a pulse of light, *time does not exist:* clocks stop at the speed of light. Thus mass and hence energy, as well as time, are born from the photon, from light, which is therefore the first kingdom, the first stage of the **process** that **engenders the universe.**
(Some bold and italic emphases are added.)

The Reflexive Universe, *Evolution of Consciousness*
Arthur M. Young, Delacorte Press/Seymour Lawrence
Published by arrangement with Robert Briggs Associates, San Francisco, CA 1976

Preface

"Every analysis of the conditions of human knowledge must rest on considerations of the character and scope of our means of communication."

Niels Bohr, Atomic Physics and Human Knowledge

What is communication? How do we communicate (both with ourselves and with others), and to what extent are we successful in communicating? What do *context* and *relationship*, and the notions of cumulative knowledge, and discovery and stimulation by way of words, have to do with the conveyance of *intent* and/or *meaning*?

I think it is fair to say that much is assumed with respect to our understanding and implementation of conventional forms of communication, (thinking and speaking), their processual means, and inherent *categories* of meaning. Honesty would seem to suggest that we acknowledge our limitations in the crucial and essential endeavor of communicatory methodology. But even thus acknowledged, what then do we do? How do we proceed?

At the outset a common (but rich and comprehensive) syntax would seem to be fundamentally and foundationally necessary, and I believe it is. But, even with reasonable agreement regarding a structural grammar, the gap between syntactical utterings and signings, and sure semantic *grokking*, is wide indeed. Somehow we need to augment the way in which we arrive at (agreed upon) meaning. And syntax, though

The Fine Structure Constant

basic, seems from experience incapable, alone, of dealing with meaning. So the question really becomes one of semantic proficiency (and with practice, perhaps, even virtuosity).

In this somewhat unconventional volume I try, by way of what I refer to as a cumulo-contextual and lexico-heuristic format of poetic philosophy, to show how experimentation with words might enrich and enhance our ability to communicate, thus helping to generate and develop a more proficient semantics. I try, through glimpses, hints, and skeptical speculations (Greek. *skeptikos* - thoughtful and reflective; Latin. *speculari* - to observe, to contemplate) to show how word/thought creativity might stimulate our ideas, improve our thinking, and thus advance interaction beyond the current state of (socially endemic) lingual prevarication.

I would further suggest that simply by being mindful of the following formulaic frames of reference and inquiry, one might perhaps be encouraged to engage in more presuppositionless thinking. This might help to significantly improve and clarify attempts at communication by limiting unverified assumptions (by posing more questions than answers). And this by itself may prove to be a major rhetorical device leading to improved interaction by inherently limiting communicatory confusion. The formulae:

> *What* constitutes the frame and/or ground? (Ontology = *what is.*)
>
> *How* do we know what we think we know? (Epistemology = *how known.*)
>
> *What* might we do (speak, sign, act, transmit, be)? (Axiology = *what should.*)

Keith Whittingslow

At any rate, there seems to be a great need to semantically stimulate our individual and collective, and philosophical and psychological, nature. And, while there may be any number of effective ways to accomplish this, in what follows I humbly offer just a few that seem to be of help to me. But, whichever heuristics might apply, let us persist in trying to evoke deep intuitional interpersonal communicatory intercourse. (Aurobindo said that intuition is but a memory of the truth.) I think we will then find that our intrapersonal (causal, teleological?) internal lingual-somatic semantics will flourish as well. It might be that the latter then catalyzes the former, which in turn expands the latter again, and so on.

The multiplistic hermeneutic gyre is thus not just set in motion. It may have *been* in motion all the while; we just didn't perceive it.

Cumulo-contextual, speculative, lexico-heuristic versification can possibly help us to see the magical implicate-explicate *logos* in all of its fullness, splendor, and totality - the endless and infinite variety of constellational kaleidoscopic forms, ideas, and ideals.

The volume presently in your hands, experimental as it may be, is my attempt at least to respond to the call outlined above.

I

Speculative-Heuristic Verse

Words as Dimensional Transforms

Words according to Huxley are the "instruments of thought; they form the channel along which thought flows; they are the molds in which thought is shaped".

Also, adds Humphrey, the reverse is true; "thoughts are the molds in which words are shaped, they form the channel along which words flow; words come into use or change their meaning as and when people have a prior idea they are striving to express".

I would add that while indeed words do change worlds, and world perceptions shape and engender words, that this reflexive process has not as yet been fully developed.

Consider the following as linguistically trance-formational.

If metaphorically Logos did indeed descend into matter (in the beginning - word - flesh, etc.,) then Yeats' notion of the double gyre (not to mention

The Fine Structure Constant

the Tao) would seem to indicate that the transference, while being not only valid, is expediently recurrent, unending, cyclical, two-way, all-pervasive, pleromatic, and profoundly relational.

Nietzsche, Bohm, Boehme, and many others are thus not only vindicated, but canonized.

So let us have words as catalysts, as music, as heuristics, as probes, as poetics, as psychotropics, as channels, molds, instruments, transforms, truths, consequences, checks, balances, queries, propositions, experiments, variances, translations, ciphers and de-ciphers.

Let us be intimate with words, thoughts, ideas, memories, gestures, meanings, and most of all imaginings.

Let us see and realize all dimensions of existence, and even of non-existence. Let us employ words to their full potential.

Let us deconstruct all conceptual frames, while experiencing nature as dynamic, open, contingent, and novel.

Let us seek dimensional transforms through the wonderment of

Words . . .

Subjectionality

Conscientious Objections/Projections

The solar wind
bathes *our* system . . .

                                      Then

breathes out further still,
to be re-inspired, reflexively
back through the membranous
alveolaroid spirit/matter *fluviae*
of this *particular* universe . . .

                                      Now

neutrinos enter our dense but
sentient bio-logical windows
after passing ghost-like through
anti-matter, black holes, and
angst-suffused/ridden gravity fed
virtual (relative) reality . . .

                                      Again

The Fine Structure Constant

    the sorgeaic center adjusts
    for akashic expansion/contraction
    and, the tensional stretch repeats
    yet another cycle ...

                            When

    indeed how, or even why - does the limit-source
    allow inter-system transformations ... ?

                            Conspirationality!
                            (breathing together)

Life, Energy, Wisdom, and Cosmos

Life   immense, eager, passionate -
     life imbued with destiny,
     fortitude, intrigue.

Energy   transfusing and permeating
     all magnificently - energy of
     measureless amplitude, generative,
     kinetic, smiling sweetly and serenely.

Wisdom   how wondrous that *sophos*
     seemingly develops with and
     through perseverance, intent
     and equanimity.

Cosmos   inexorable, reflexive,
     effulgent, and refluent by way of exquisitely
     infinite systems, and dormancy,
     and recuperative silence.

Re-Cognizing and Re-Membering

Somehow, we are an accumulation
of happenings, experiences, sufferings
and joys that have been, are being, and
will be.

At times, we reflect upon some of these
events, but always there is a horizon
beyond which we cannot see or remember.

Perhaps the goal, the end point -
enlightenment - is when we can hold *all*
experience in the present moment.

This fullness of memory (presence of mind) -
as reality *now* - obliterates the event-horizon
(which was only an illusion anyway; no matter
that it is developmentally *real* for humans -
and thus in a certain context does *matter*).

Finally, somehow we might understand (to the
extent that it can be cognized) or, more appropriately,
be able to see and to feel a continuum of light *and* dark,
as one *and* many.

This re-joining/re-membering - bringing all
of the parts back together (resolving dis-memberment)
might, over time, prove to be the fullest expression of ...

integration.

A Socratic Koan

First, recall a traditional koan ... e.g.,

> We know the sound
> of two hands clapping.
> But, what is the sound
> of one hand clapping?

Then, consider and contemplate the following ...

> We know, generally, the result/effect
> of one person employing
> Socratic method conversationally
> with/upon another person.
> But, what results when
> two people employ simultaneously
> Socratic method conversationally
> with/upon each other ...

silence.

Sourceology

∴
photons
create

nuclear   proton
particles   ℘   electron

generating mass and charge
basic substance of the universe

in contradistinction to
the
light
that created
them

but . . .

ratio, meaning, angle   condensation

≠

activity   mass

1/137
(the fine structure constant)
remains

uncommitted   free

The Fine Structure Constant

ever　　　　　　　　　　*dimensionless*　　　　　　　　　　never

uncertainty of position and momentum are manifest
in what
we
see
as fundamental particles

to observe a photon is to annihilate it
leaving nothing left to predict

even so . . . it is posited that
particle observation induces uncertainty and is ∴ epistemological

&

implicit in the definition of the fine structure constant
particles are *innately* uncertain and are ∴ also ontological

Σ　　　　　　　　　　　　　　$\int$

gnomonic　　　　mnemonic　　　　no manic
physics　　　　　　　　　　　psychics

∞

semper　　　　　　　ψ　　　　　　　*liberalis*

The Fine Structure Constant

There is a nodal dwelling place
somewhere
out
among
spiraling,
expanding
galactic ramparts.

Parts of me
rest
there,
weightless
within elegant,
crystalline
geometrically precise
snowflake-shaped
islands.

Other parts of me
disperse
into
hyperspace
through a network
of

The Fine Structure Constant

shimmering
prisms,
by way of
pervasive analogical
xylem and phloem
emanating tumultuously
like the roar
of
a
tiger,
and
softly
like the breath
of
a
lotus.

Between
time and not-time
I stretch, soar
and glide,
as I pass through
a phase-dimensional
emblazoned patina
of
free
pure
unbound
energy.

Keith Whittingslow

This interplay is
simply . . .
force.

It is
true,
graceful,
gleaming, boundless,
unconditional and indecipherable.

It is not a
thing.
They are myriad
glistening, all-permeating,
mirage-suffused,
amorphous
resonant
visual glissandi.

They
are
poles
of
a
force field,
that derive
there seeming
         oppositeness
and
         otherness
from
         chirality.

The Fine Structure Constant

The
fine structure constant
is the pulse
of
certainty, *will* and *dominion*.
These entities
are
vortices:
nature's most basic
sensuality;
because vortices are
consubstantial
with
their matrix . . .
the *surround*.

While spinning
as
vortices,
I - they - we
crossover
inexorably
through
icy shadows
and
heat-blasted
stark
wind-forged, wave-washed,
bold,
vast reaches of . . . Tao.

Keith Whittingslow

We exist
self-reflexively
in ever-changing
format,
imbued with radiance
like the sky,
like a corolla,
like a super-nova,
like the aura of
ionic consciousness
rising
from
an endless
desert
horizon.

Vortical motion
has been
and
always will be
inexplicable
like the
purring of cats,
the melodies of birds,
and
the
singing of cetaceae.

The fine structure constant
splits into
parts

The Fine Structure Constant

     while
remaining whole.
The fine structure constant
is
     forever
          free,
it is interdimensional,
polyphonic
and
synaesthetic.

The fine structure constant
is like the
burst
of
loveliness
from the center
of a rosebud,
the sheen
of a dew drop,
the rainbow-spectralized
spray of the shining sea,
the will and intentionality
inherent
in all wave forms,
the dream that
engenders
a
universe ... *creation.*

Indeed, the indwelling,
enfolded, interpenetrating

Keith Whittingslow

double-gyre,
which always
moves through,
toward,
and from itself,
signifies
the *mind*
which can only be
symbolized by
our notions of
vortices, expressed and functioning
as the fine structure constant.

I, you, we, us . . .
enthralled
and
spellbound . . .
through each breath
and
pulse . . .
cast an infinite network of *vortices* . . .
the
force
and
simultaneity
of which . . .
is
both
being
and
becoming.

The Core

Memory might be angularly analogous
> to the anatomy of
> an alleged anomaly.

Coruscative metonyms oft times implode
> with meaning, as in ***all meaning
> is an angle,*** while affinities
> occupy places seemingly eternally
> . . . from here to infinity.

Rain permeates the Cosmos' interstitae;
> light before and after sleep
> colors life's microtudes,
> and *vice versa.*

Interpretations may be interspersed incrementally;
> the cell wall construes the body's
> contextually quotidian concavities.

Language dissipates simultaneous negentropic representations,
> scooping peaches in convex oval cups
> and blue-yellow buckets.

Keith Whittingslow

Time's descriptors rest on breast,
    head, mind and soul,
        perceptively, yet sexually processual.

Communicatory motes excrete tree-like
    branches of being.

Poems may, or may not
    have consciences.

Space contains, and is contained in,
    the consciously unconscious set,
    which contains within it
    the set of all sets, as well as
    the set containing no sets.

The core begets the cell,
    the cell expands reflexively,
    knowledge begets understanding,
    the cell deconstructs,
    light returns,
    the fine structure constant
    retrieves its lost parts.

Core freedoms come and go,
    cell-like.

Celestial Resonance

Dancing the not-two step
we all jam own variation
of the infinite vibratory theme.

Some are prism-like
and reflect the archetypal
holographic image - *Roy G. Biv.*

Some are transducers
whose quasi-phononical
feeling tones are the stepped down,
edited, raw first draft of intuitive pulse.

Some are vortices who
analyze/synthesize bioelectric
oscillatory circuitry, and meld
reciprocally nested crosstalk.

We are all shards of the
great cloud that materializes,

Keith Whittingslow

and dematerializes, and that is
at once known and unknown.

We are toroidal dew drops
who slip into and out of
the great shining sea.

We are all recombinant *elfs*
who by way of *e/l freq.*, spin, roll,
charm, phase and re-create
the essential quantum ontological
matrix that is ever present
and is spectrally *you*-biquitous.

The Wind at Djemila

Remembering Camus

The warmth

of knowing

you

shall perpetuate

the

glow of life

within my

soul

even though my

mind

might steal away the

Keith Whittingslow

    sun

and leave my

  heart

cold and still.

Exoteric/Esoteric

As I sit
in
my garden,
my vision replicates
wonders
of translucency.

Endless gradations
of
color parade
back and forth
between
the source
and
my gray, impressionable
mediatory
organum transducere.

Light's functional wave collapses,
beckoning spontaneously,
while simultaneously
conveying
voluminous, dancing,
dark, light, blue, green
representational variations.

Keith Whittingslow

The vast continuum fills
my
field of view,
at once finite,
yet
paradoxically pleromatic.

Manifold gyrations
bridge
the diaphanous, interstitial passageways
between (and within)
the boundless, vertiginous
stream of explicate
lucidity.

The deep recesses
of
mammoth pines,
I know to be
green,
yet appear black.

The near, middle and far
space
is
a delirious, deliquescent
and scintillating blueness.

Leaves
seem to generate

The Fine Structure Constant

an
internal brilliance,
radiating a deep, liquid,
blinding
yet
soul-penetrating-quenching greenness.

I equivocate,
by way of
internal dialogue,
as I contemplate
the spectacle
which
absorbs me,
that which we call universe
. . . omniscience.

All seminal perceptions
fall victim
to
comparative interpretations;
perspective
is
arbitrary
and
abstract.

Differences and distinctions
inaccurately represent
an *ignis fatuus,*
neti neti,
fluvial, processual universe.

Keith Whittingslow

Color, form,
warp, woof,
pour, image,
marking and situation
cannot be consistently,
reliably,
or equitably replicated.

Reproductions
of
primal forms
are
imaginal inventions ... phantoms.

Nonetheless,
these fictions
although
metaphoric and symbolic,
are
ciphers
and
mirrors
to the one and the many,
the inside and the outside,
and ...
the blue and the green.

They continually
and
luminously
transpose both darkness and light

The Fine Structure Constant

from
temporal,
unending
ineffabilities,
to
momentary
yet
meaningful
blessed
bits
of
perspicuity.

Winter Solstice

With precision and affirmation the sun slowly wheels and turns, thus renewing its upward journey, once again fulfilling the promise of light, warmth and regeneration.

Its life-giving-sustaining process is akin to the sea-lion's skin; seamless, like the moebius wrappings of the cosmos. Its implicate-explicate enfoldment forever revolving; undulating, seemingly involuted, yet emerging anew into familiar yet ever-novel topographies.

There is a tacit, objectively unverifiable knowing in the solstice event(s), the pinne-ped's aqua-sleek form-motion, and the toroidally inter-linked extensions between the experiential ground and the apparent yet deceptive(?) limitless horizon.

The Fine Structure Constant

Let us ponder the mystery of suns, and seals -
and all wild creatures (humans included) who
pulse and resonate to/with the sidereal music
of the universe.

Still, yet flowing; quiet, yet sonorous; present, yet
unfolding; existing, yet emerging; being, yet becoming;
let us feel the rhythm, and sway inwardly yet pleromatically,
as we dance forever, to-with-in nature's essence.

Snarl

*S*uchness?

*N*othingness!

*A*ridity!?

*R*ecursivity!?!?

*L*amentableness.

Quantum Etheric Cosmology

Rave on Doctor Chew

Circular (meaningful) / repetitive de(con)struction
shapes/vectors evolution of non-space/time from matter.
Ialdabaothic recursive tautologies bootstrap and
reassemble the Abraxic hermeneutic/phenomenological
sphere imprinted upon/within the matrix and the
interstitae of the Trismegistic Hermetic Emerald Tablet.

Particulate vortices collide and thus fall,
isolating Aeons, Archons and category errors
in multifarious combinatory milieux.

The demiurgically generated pseudo energy, ersatz space,
and non-real time representations depend on
perpetually/perceptually filtered, lens distorted
interpretations (endarkenment).

Condensational, phase dimensional decompressions
have natural evolution creation generator capability;
bi-linear annihilation operators have expectation value;

Keith Whittingslow

classical systems dynamics fluctuate quantum-mechanically
as functions set-wise, within temporal/isolated
(withdrawn-from) empty/entropic space.

Non-classical informal (atuxal) processes strunction
co-creatively/co-existentially within *and* without
the non-representational multiple bageloid/toroidal
pleroma of tutti-frutti.

Chew your words carefully Geoffrey ChawSir.

The Whole Enchilada

Re-Membering it in Bytes and Peaces

We knew *it* . . . . but we forgot *it*.

We plunged deliriously into the
burning blue-green abyss,
that drew us in/outward, to
what seemed like **the** expedient
Lila/sport-play/experience.

And then we were lost.

We struggled, groped, clawed and
thought our way through the
quasi-substantoid, matter/strata of being.

Glimpses, hints and clues (pre-positioned?)
indicated that we must traverse the
long, slow spectral arc of involution/evolution.

But something told us that
logico-sci-tech-ops, were not
Taoic divinitoid processes.

Keith Whittingslow

We sensed that pre-personal pleromatic
Eden precedes egoic existenuum, and
leads ultimately to trans-personal paradise.

Even so, we fiddle today with
electro-taco-chips and computer (retrieval?)
control, thinking that we can arrive at
reign-baeux end by way of
secular-servo-machinations.

Perhaps we will come to re-cognize ...
again, and *again*, and *again* ... that the
sphere-space-point, macro-micro, all/nothing,
now-forever *stuff,* is the realativistic
inspire-ational breath of divine blown-out
love/peace.

O Felix Culpa

Could Einstein have been wrong ... does (a) God play dice with the universe?

Post-modern cosmology offers data such that all good/evil polarities might be interpreted as innumerable kaleidoscopic chips that forever fall into an endless series of ever differing forms.

There might also be, it seems likely, eternal archetypal ideas and forms; but the *earthly format* by its fullest definition and expression encompasses a recurring scenario which casts *homo mundanus* into the role of deceptively mutable yet eternally suffering, experimental laboratory animals.

Does this (reckoned by human ideals) de[in]humanization, this experimental vivisection, ultimately evolve from evil, squalor and lies, to beauty, goodness and truth?

Or, does it simply fulfill a continuing round of (human) meaninglessness, while at the same time satisfying the maniacally driven sport-play needs of a robotic saturnine impersonal gargoloid unfeeling cosmic mutant demiurge?

Alain Aspect's twin *knowing* particles would seem to indicate an intelligent, possibly even a purposeful and meaningful universe. But additional evidence, experience and knowledge (as opposed to belief) are needed if we are to understand and/or countervail present obvious thanatism.

G[4] R[3] I[2] N[1]

Gnosis and grace ... grant goodness;

return, requiescence and resolution;

infinite ... indissoluble

nature.

The Evolution of Consciousness

A Two Stage Symbiosis

Alice Bailey had it right. So did Plato, Aquinas, Steiner, Brunton, Blavatsky, McDermott, Tarnas, and especially Ken Wilbur.

Intellect, in a major sense, must precede intuition.

Ultimately a *cumulo contextual, lexico heuristic*, hierarchical and rigorous knowing will operate simultaneously with a personal contemplative/meditative process of inner visioning. One without the other is sterile, misleading, eternally distorted, and hopelessly fragmented, resulting in a quasi-permanent lodging in a samsara-like round of stale bio-processual reruns.

A comprehensive approach to becoming is essential. Indeed, Wilbur outlines the process best in advocating philosophical/psychosocial virtuosity, coupled with a lengthy program of Zazen (sitting) contemplation. Along the way the major deterrents remain: category error, the pre-trans fallacy, legitimacy vs. authenticity, structure-stage confusion, and premature closure.

Thus, my allegorical gestalt in terms of the free will/determinism fundamentum, is that the fuel for the *processual* evolution of consciousness is a two-stage elemental/essential/ existential symbiotic admixture, neither part of which will activate without the other. One

The Fine Structure Constant

is inherent momentum, a *pull from above* if you will; the other is autogenic, that is to say that part of the monad (that which comes before the soul and continues throughout) must *kick in* or bootstrap, or self-catalyze *intentionally.* Employing the *light* metaphor, we can think of ourselves as prismatic/channels that the free causal light flows through to become spectralized/manifested. But, it is up to us to *position* ourselves properly and accurately, in order to receive and *process* the light through our being, and thus truly experience *integration.*

The Trap

Matter, Earth and the Feminine

It seems that Sophia jumped the gun;
existence perforce *began* unsound.
Earth's vast predicaments thus are spun,
in dense matter and dull ground.

The earth **is** feminine,
to be sure;
but to not re-examine
is *the* deadly lure.

To know the Logos, the eternal spark,
requires true gnosis of one's self;
but, to pierce the veil of matter dark,
one must not enlist the *other's* help.

Donne, Blake and Yeats all knew,
there's but one way to alter fate;
the valley dragon must be slew,
that solves the riddle, and opens the gate.

The Fine Structure Constant

Again, Nietzsche's strange claim
is clear, when seen in proper light;
Sophia still suffers with her shame,
and knowledge alone can set things right.

Icebergs in Outer Space

Inter-human communicational proficiency?
Inadequate.

Analogy:
Visualize sad, unknowing, unfeeling, mute, icy blue lumps
floating silently in deep, cold, unconscious, vast, endless space.

Gaia ...
schmaia.

What's the answer?
First, we must formulate meaningful questions.
Does the abyss widen?
Is the universe *closed*, or *open*?
Does it matter? [physical matter? or metaphysical relevance?]

The Fine Structure Constant

Hope?
         Perhaps.

Progress?
         No supportable evidence, thus far.

Transparencies

…light…

from	trans	parere	parabolic
within	across/through	appear	lumen(es)sense

              to   two   too

TAO

earth	t'ai chi	prism
ray	way	sun

>*property of light transmittance enables bodies to be seen through* <

human   OPALESCENCE   notwithstanding

      transpicuous   *waves*

The Fine Structure Constant

    penetrate   sheer   pellucid   bright
       clear   pierce   pervious   free

fine texture open mesh

akashic

paradox   paragon   paradigm

tranquil
transfigure
beguile
guileless
disguise
pretenseless
prehensile
prehension

dis-cover   evident   beyond   perfect
   open   dis-closure   transform   true

eukukleos   *Aletheie*

trans-spire
con-spire
breath
death
earth
dance
trance
enhance

Keith Whittingslow

meta   empsychoun
over   animate

                metempsychosis

soul   transmigration

   solely   severalty

     across   through

…light…

Some Names, Attributes, and/or Characteristics of the Numinous

Angel Fire ...

You, me, we, it ... the monad, the totality, the force, archetype, metaphor, image, symbol, Ontos, allegory, zeit geist, kundalini, akasha, purusa/prakriti, spirit, Brahman, Siva/Sakti, Vishnu, Atman, samadhi, moksha.

Blue Wave ...

Omniverse, cosmos, group soul, universal mind, Self, heart, matrix, source, point*space holostalt, nirvana, sunyata, satori, yin-yang, Tao, light, essence, dasein, Osiris, Seth, Thoth, Ra, Odin, consciousness, elan vital.

Green Serpent ...

Ahriman, Ormazd, pneuma, psyche, torus, chaos, process, dream time, Dominion, space, void, fullness, ground/chain of being, emptiness, Yahwe, Ayin, Shekhinah, Abba/Amma, Abraxas, Sophia,

Lucifer, Ialdabaoth, Mephistopheles, the unnamable, ineffable, abyss.

Violet Pearl ...

Maya, Lila, flux, causal, absolute, fount, primality, intuitiae, awareness, knowing, grace, Truth, purity, freedom, breath, resonance, mercy, Buddha, Zoroaster, Mani, Krishna, Christ, Mohammed, nature, physis, magic, kinesis, life, gnosis, philos, agape, Love.

Angel Fire ... Blue Wave ... Green Serpent ... Violet Pearl you ... me ... we ... it .... Numena.

The Dream

I have experienced one
dream,
singularly unique ...
unlike any other
dream,
either previous or subsequent.

The quality of the
images,
the entire texture of the
visualization ...
radically different from any
dream,
before or since.

There was a shimmering
electric quality,
neither surreal nor ethereal, but
hyper-real
in appearance.

The *stuff* of the
seeing ...
was much more

Keith Whittingslow

alive ...
than any prior experience,
or any since.

There was a
brilliance,
a pulsing,
an ingenuousness ...
to say that it was quintessentially
vivid
would be to completely understate.

The light and the color
were exceedingly
vital,
full,
rich.

It is difficult to describe the
intensity, the voluminosity,
the quality ...
that I saw.

Essentially,
I recall seeing several
things;
a fish-like structure,
then grass?
or seaweed?

In turn,
each of these

The Fine Structure Constant

objects
would undergo a
process
of
transformation ...
which I can only
describe
as disintegration;
but ... slowly ...
that is, the imagery
both traversed and negated
time ...
all the while
scintillating,
glowing,
pulsating ...
then gradually phasing
or fading (inadequate descriptors),
down to ultimate
disappearance.

However, it seemed
important
that just before
phasing/fading
out
completely,
the visualization
phased down to a
core
something or other.

Keith Whittingslow

This core
essence
was not well-defined,
but something
made it seem
crucially
significant,
as if this was the
real
heart
of the
imagery,
or message.

Again, the cycle ...
flourishing,
radiant things
that then
quiver, and slowly
phase down to disappear
and disintegrate ...
after showing a
core
essence.

It was not clear
if the core essence
actually
disappeared/disintegrated,
but the implication was of a
phasing
over/into

The Fine Structure Constant

another cycle....
another reintegration (?) ...
somewhere/somewhen ... else?

The intellectual conceptualization that I
infer
from the dream
has to do with both the symbol (objectification)
and the metaphor (process) of
sunyata ...
the void, the flux,
the constant
ebb and flow and ...
creation/destruction
of the
uni/holoverse;
the void being ... not void, as commonly
conceived,
but in fact ...
full;
or paradoxically,
full *and* empty simultaneously.

In sum, this single
dream
was in a certain
sense
a breakthrough of sorts.

I continue to
hope

Keith Whittingslow

that it represents a
beginning,
or an
opening,
towards ever-new
seeings.

I wait and
search
eagerly,
breathlessly, yet
patiently
in anticipation ...
of someday experiencing another
dream,
which hints, however minimally, as before at
inner vision,
and a fuller
reality ...
and seeming
importance.

Summer Solstice

Suspended, amaranthine, and ostensibly still at its zenith;
the sun imperceptibly, yet resolutely continues to spiral
through the enfolding, unfolding, omniversal multiplistic gyre.

The spectacle repeats the illusion of warmth, light, fullness,
and wellness; but, it also betells the non-apodictic
shining-effulgent, dark-dull *janus pneumaticos*.

The quasi-logic and cognitive sense of vast, cyclical,
rhythmic perturbations bespeaks an inherent eternal caveat;
which is that pleromatic benevolence and ontological essence
are but one-half of the toroidal admixture, infinitely
balanced out by (and embedded in) the mist of Indra's
reflexive, photovoltaic, sunyatic, ayinic net.

Only those who totally recall nature's awe-full, fluctual
disparate parity, will safely transit the many worlds,
evincing an enigmatic smile, all the while humming softly
to *themselves;* for, strange but true, there is no *other* one
to whom to sing.

The mystery is unsolvable, but it is livable; paradox,
irony, parsimony, tantra, *and* the gnostic razor of Ockham,
are keys that both lock and unlock the cosmic koan.

Keith Whittingslow

Conscious agents must responsibly decide which way to position both lock and key; or, where the peripheral center is, around which *all* suns revolve; and, that the only fixed absolute, is that there are no fixed absolutes.

One, or an infinite number of Goedel's sets, yields the same unvarying existential variant; that objectless consciousness is, by and large, unconsciously incomplete.

Molte Colore

She has many names, forms, personas
and hues.

She appeared to me for the first time
late at night during my walk along
the ridge.

Ragged, yet valiant; abandoned, yet
courageous. She had only a dry creak
for a voice. But she was trusting
and eager for companionship.

Starving, she accepted my midnight bowls
and morsels.

As summer turned wintry, she gladly
took cover in a box that I placed
in her wild habitat.

Keith Whittingslow

Then when icy rains set in, she very
cautiously followed me home.

X-rays revealed that her back had been
broken. She had received cruel maltreatment.

I nicknamed her MC after reporting the first
sighting to my wife a *multi-colored cat!*

Despite her travails, she retains the
sweet, devoted, playful and intimate
persona that must be characteristic
of Maine Coon tabbies.

Coincidental with Pat's Italian lessons,
MC officially became Molte Colore (Many
Colors).

Yet I like to think that MC is my
spirit-guide appearing to me in cat form;
and thus she's Metaphysical Cat, along
with numerous additional sobriquets ...
Magical Cat, Mystery Cat, Magnificat, etc.,
etc.

The Fine Structure Constant

MC has been with us almost eight years now, and our lives continue to be enhanced, and entranced by her unending sagacity, grace and charm.

She is truly a magnanimous creature.

Lucid Breathing

The Stillpoint of Intercosmic Connectivity
A Prescription for Mantric/Mandalic Re-Spiration

Rx: Elixir Akasha

In ... ad proximus ... en-spiritus;

That which is inspired co-constitutes
golden energy filled threads/braids of
light which suffuse, activate, pulse, permeate,
pervade, resonate and illuminate; imparting
life, being and completeness. Effulgent
fullness, solace, con-solidarity and tranquil
all/isness result.

Ritorno Explicatus

Out ... ad distalis ... ex-spiritus;

That which is expired takes the form/image
of super-fine crystalline particle mist,
sparkling jewel-like, brilliant, multi-colored,
and kaleidoscopic; shimmering, glowing and reflecting
omni-dimensional, rainbow-hued bits of ever expanding

The Fine Structure Constant

serene radiance.

Ritorno Implicatus

Repeat the cycle as needed and as appropriate.

The Stoker

Bio/Thanatic Re-Genesis

Somatically/soulfully soaring through
ten miles of wooded hills; the pre-ignition
of complex carbohydrates
and vital amines
fuels and fuses the psycho-re-cognition of
the reticular activating notochord.

Awash with neurotransmitters,
stoked with, and soaked in endorphins;
knoshing on neologisms,
the *I* within and without
contemplates the inchoate/metabolic self.

Biochemophysiobehavioral phenomena
swarm, swirl and catalyze
the furnace in my cosmic core;
I self-bootstrap into multiple metaphysical
recursive/reflexive cyclical feedback loops.

Psychoneuroontologically flushed
and glowing with maximum brilliance,
I radiate pure energy
at the mind/body junctional interface.

The Fine Structure Constant

Approaching total and absolute
time, space, distance
warp/escape velocity,
I am at once, simultaneously, both spirit consciousness
and subtly-ambulatory-psychotic.

Nascently, I rise from the ashes . . . a dis-negentropic
chimera,
both now *and* at the hour of my death.

Process, Truth, and Provisionality

Means to an end? fluxual ... multi-versal ... processual;

contextually/categorically bound ... theory soaked ...

mediated;

paradox ... irony ... inherent (deterministic?) plurality;

wish (fantasy) fulfillment ... self-fulfilling ... (belief laden)

prophecy;

validity and means ... reverent skepticism ... enthrallment

contingency;

evil -> existentialism -> enlightenment;

being ... becoming ... comprehensivity ... structure stage confusion

legitimacy

authenticity

The Fine Structure Constant

pre-trans category error/fallacy;

psycho-social moral/ethical duty ... relational equanimity ... dynamic colloidality

inconsistent ... uncoordinated ... incoherent;

interpretation ... perspective ... concept/percept

anthropomorphic projections;

here and now ... where and when ... who and what ... why

intransigent perturbations;

nothing makes sense without philosophy;

belief ... no   faith ... no

hope ... maybe

The Double-Truth Universe
The Western Mind's Predicament

Through the linear Copernican, Cartesian, Kantian thought progression devolved the Western weltanschauung; from a Platonic ideal of wholeness towards a pluralistically fragmented, psychologically expedient, multi-versally precipitated, suspensional cosmic colloid.

Ockham's razor limned the initial perforational bifurcation whose excoriations adumbrated the scientific/secular revolution that would rent the Thomistic synthesis, the divine ontological oestrus, asunder into an Orwellian *via moderna* in which cosmological alienation would become increasingly compounded by epistemological nihilism.

All human understanding became as dysfunctional subsets of interpretive analysis. No interpretation was, or is, ever final.

God became a LaPlacian *unnecessary hypothesis.*

The (known) universe continues to yield partial, elusive, and conflicting information. Yet it offers/allows no degree of human control. Is there a resolution to this seemingly vicious and pernicious double-bind? Do we have a (redemptive) card to play that is as yet unknown to us?

What drives the process? Is there a (wave/particle) complementarity between autogenicity and cosmic *pull? Is* there even a *process?*

The Fine Structure Constant

Small wonder that many presently worry anxiously whether we are temporarily, or eternally, caught in the chaotic dimensional swirl of entropic heat death (teleologically analagous to *Kali Yuga?*). Or are we arriving at a transduction point between epochal aeonic dimensions — a pivotal linking of the biological and the archetypal? Are we approaching a *hieros gamos*, a sacred marriage? [Richard Tarnas indicates that the infinite masculine is re-cognizing and re-emerging into the eternal feminine — the omega point of — *life.*]

But, reason dictates continuing serious doubt. And we may yet be, for all *intent* and *purpose* on a round-trip journey, from nowhere to nothingness.

The Edge

Between Prose and Poetry

On the edge; this seems to be not only how we live sometimes, but perhaps, what we need to do more of. It is a question of, as Bugenthal says, 'philosophic venturing.' It is *the* issue. It is the *challenge* to find out who and what we really are. It is learning to effect the merger of intuition and reason. It is learning how to enhance the existential/ transpersonal interface, how to catalyze state-altering potential. It is to challenge (and be willing to change) every currently held belief, faith, and feeling. It is to be diligent steadfast, eager and *anxious,* to *generate* self-development, through self-analysis. It is to deal seriously with existential - phenomenological issues - ultimate concerns. It is to recognize that humanity is

The Fine Structure Constant

presently limited in awareness, process, and perception. But also that humanity is dynamic and seems to have potential for change and unfoldment (blossoming). It is to see that we are living 'contingently,' because we are in a position of dealing with a vast number of unknowns. We have an insufficient data base (at least we have difficulty in actualizing the *real* data, even though it may be 'there' or 'here,' awaiting uncovering). It is to increase this 'data base,' to reflexively 'see' more of what existence and being really are about. It is to make certain adjustments, in attitude, in vision, in perception, interpretation - to learn how to become 'open' to the energy and vibrations that resonate everywhere. It is to tune our being (antennae-receiver) to be able to access the energy and vibrational level that abounds in the ether. It is to effect the existential crisis, day by day, hour by hour, minute by minute, second by second, to *live* it. If we seem stuck, it may be because we need to go 'down' further, before we can come 'up.' It is to be eager to *choose* to expand, to know, to love, to care, (to help one's self only to be able to help others). It is to *seek* and *attain* optimality. It is to progress from the existential level, transcendentally, to the causal-absolute level. It is to live, to be, to exist - *on the edge*.

Toccata Gnostica Semantica

To touch, to know, to understand . . .
the meaning of it all.
This is the essential quest.

Is there a **tertium quid,**
beyond rationality, yet vastly more satisfying
than the stale, dim, subliminal representational
detritus of contemplation, meditation and prayer?

How to experience that *brilliant composition*
in free form, the incongruous phantasm of
imagination that winks deceptively
at/from/on the distant margins of our perception,
tantalizing and tempting, yet remaining forever
illusory and insubstantial? The *creativa positiva*
without *semantica* is explicitly pointless and thus
negativa.

The *magica semantica* may only be
knowable through a wisdom loving *gnostica,*
which itself may only be enacted/engendered by way of
a *via speculativa,* which is so
precarious in/by nature, that the barest hint of
delimitation (belief in, or naming as solid truth)

instantaneously and irrevocably distorts and blocks
forever the true *lux perpetuosa*.

Let the *magica* that is the music of the spheres
allow us to *speculate* purely and simply, and to
know fully and finally the *Toccata Gnostica Semantica*.

A Meditation

A mandala, with many forms and
variations ...
which can account for
oneness,
in addition to
manyness;
finiteness
and
indefiniteness;
atemporalness,
and
pantemporalness.

It appears to have
beginnings
and
endings,
but at the same time is a
continuum ... (cyclical).

It is light (first cause),
energy/vibration (Aum)
filled ...
yet, channel-like, *empty, lacunae* and/or

dispersed
as the yield of one, or many colors, is dependent upon
prismatic
ingress, or
egress.

It has a central
axis,
as well as an infinite number of microid central
axes.

This mandala begins with a
visualization
of the fundamental strunction (structure +
function) of a
torus ...
but this toroidal format undergoes
dynamic
processual
change.

The encased portion of the
hypersphere (the first of multiple paradoxes),
expands significantly, and the middle,
doughnut-hole becomes shrunken, or de-
emphasized.

Not until the image is substantially
developed, and
seen

The Fine Structure Constant

more fully, can the hole or middle be
conceived of,
comprehended,
cognized, or
actualized.

Initially, the hypersphere, or
torus,
is seen as having a transparent,
filmy-like surface, and its structure and substance
seem not unlike a child's soap bubble.

It then begins an expansion-like
process,
but in addition the surface is seen to
swirl
in a uniform fashion
distally ... (away from the center).

This is at first problematical,
because as yet there is no sense
of there being a
center!

Then the realization dawns
that the only way that
this can continue is that there
must be a central tube or passageway
so that the surface can move
from apparent start to apparent finish —
ad infinitum.

Keith Whittingslow

And then, a further
realization occurs:
that there is no starting point,
or finishing point, that not only
does *it* rotate, spread, expand,
and contract, but it does so
forever,
without end —
it doesn't ever start,
and it doesn't ever stop,
it just appears to flow,
and ebb —
eternally and infinitely.

One can elect,
consciously to
begin
and
end
the
mandala
wherever (at whatever stage of development)
one chooses, and also
one can thus decide,
consciously
how *much* one wants to
see (and/or interpret).

A caveat, however:
it must be determined by the
meditator,

The Fine Structure Constant

how, or to what
extent,
the issues of edgeness (as in partiality and/or
fragmentary)
are to be dealt with.

Does one control the drift,
or succumb to the flow?

Or, does the razor's edge encompass all polarity?
And, vice versa?

Are these visualizations apt metaphors for
human beingness (or becomingness)?

A clue ... (borrowed from Bob Monroe) ...

"Pas de Lieu Rhône que Nous" ... (say it
phonetically to yourself, in faster and faster
repetitions).

Japhy Ryder

      Reed   ride   road   rode

                        rails

Piute   mute   afoot   loose   muse

                      moot

JK   AG   LF   CO   RC   KR   RD   AW

[Dharma Bums?…indeed!]

Kyoto~~~~~~~~~~Kai~~~~~~~~~~you~~~~~~~~~~too

                  <sails on
                  Sappa Creek
                  in between>

Zen   Gen

                      then

metaphors   metamorphs   meditations

The Fine Structure Constant

                mediations

     ruminations   rumblings   remnants

meadows   me doze?   mud grass

lean-to   low tide   lotsa us   lo ts'us

                   lotus

                 Lao Tze

catnap   catwalk   catapult   catalyst

    caterwaul   Callicotte   *catena*

       coyote   *cognoscenti*

   cats   Catullus   lull   us

udorn   Uthant   universe   undone

    done   Donne

mew   *mu*   [Nansen]   yew   you

   you've   wove

weave   we've   Wave   brave   break

bleak   Blake   blade   bleed

Keith Whittingslow

blood/brood

mood   mode   moored   mourn

morn   orb   robe

all be   albeit   and   Albion

sundaughter   moonstar

hoary Zen

horizon

your reason

Urizen

sea   Sierra   see   are ya?

terra   tiara

saw   [long-in-the]   tooth

truth

build   write   grow   home

sow

snow   sky   rock   water

The Fine Structure Constant

    pine   bark   leaf

sigh   nigh   deer   dear

Snyder

Gaia   aerie   rheos   why?

      gray   wiry

Gary

skin   grin   bone   hair

rip rap   scat trap

Kitkitdizze

nurture

nature

no,

so?

Air Fare

Terminal Dis-ease

Terminal departure,
Deadly weights .... bags
in hand, under arms,
and under eyes.

Terminal shuffle,
Endless corridors .... concourse
gait, gate-paralysis, lizard-
breath lounge, mind pollution,
death by Muzak.

Terminal lines,
Waiting forever .... hurry
and stand, enter the vortex,
descend the Jet-Way into
the pit of inhumanity.

Terminal tubes,
Crammed and strait-jacketed .... jammed
anchovy-like, canned and stufficated;
'sit back and relax' with a curdled cocktail,
a putrid peanut, and a botuloid burrito.

The Fine Structure Constant

Terminal arrival,
Herd-like throngs .... eternal
baggage-go-round, another wait,
another line, another samsaric-shuttle
to the ends of the earth—at last! a car,
and some semblance of privacy and
self-directional determination, but
then ....

Terminal lodging,
Late night check in .... bags,
shuffle, corridors, sealed cubicles,
re-cycled cigarette air,
din of freeway, elevator, ice-
machine, and neighboring TV.

Terminal depression,
Explosive angst,
EMERGENCY RELEASE .... exigent
exit—bags flung through sealed panes;
pained person follows in dive to air, openness,
freedom .... and terminal quietude.

The Home Office

Question:

At work, when undistracted, in the privacy of his (home) office, the undersigned…

a) Talks to (and answers) himself.

b) Engages cat, dialectically (which requires, and elicits, intelligent response) in the finer points of philosophical speculation.

c) Contemplates (vacillates/equivocates) the nature, condition, reality, and wherewithal of (at least) ten thousand things.

d) Awaits/seeks intuition/inspiration regarding what his inner and outer *metier* might be.

e) Alternatingly (and/or simultaneously) laughs, cries, exults, mopes, meditates, naps.

f) Occasionally (very) conducts "business" on phone.

g) Waits patiently, and/or desperately, according to the moment, for (metaphorically speaking) Godot/godot (god/God…*oh?!?!*)

h) All of the above.

The Fine Structure Constant

i) None of the above.

J) *Both* all of the above, *and* none of the above.

Answer:

x) There is no fixed answer. All questions and answers are so to say, in oversional, contingent, and relative, and depend solely upon the minditude of the interactors. In this particular domain, however, most utterance stresponses can best be characterized by either yawns and/or meows.

Cascade

The mind's web-like linguistico-semantic interpenetrations successively elude the brain's tendency towards entropically driven downward-spiraling neuro-hormonal/electro-chemical decay.

Moreover, the will to comprehend endures and thus redirects *both* inherently chaotic ever-recurring substantive (objective) quanta *and* ever-evolving (subjective) sentient qualia.

Dimensionaloid events project glyphically and dynamically as factions of creature constituted creations (fictions) while struggling to resist untold tautological "apparent world" articles of faith.

Within psychologically prejudiced and presupposed perspectives (to the extent that they are consciously and/or unconsciously stipulated) lie implicitly embedded translational interpretations.

The Fine Structure Constant

Causa efficiens calculably exist alongside submerged pathos, sensually deprived/depraved sufferings, and occasionally emerging (yet formulaicly formed) functional forces.

Mere semeiotics and unreal (unknown and unproven) theories stultify even the most precise and careful human attempts to systematically arrange a union of essences, ideas, effects, affects, moments, and meanings.

Each event-horizon seemingly seeks all progressively and distally driven hypotheses.

Each *causa finalis* is a multiverse of many maps relationally and contextually flooding the already supersaturated sensation-warped subject.

As we strive toward a measure of stability and light, we must consequently conceive a conditional yet climactic *simulacra* in which equilibrium *flows* willfully and representationally (though symbiotically) *with* an intentionally inspired and conspired cascade of comprehension.

Gliding

I imbibe the strong dark tea
for its qualities, and powers to act
as a psychotropic *ontotheotrope* ...
an agent enabling one to experience
the magical matrix; that which constitutes
the whole.

I cross the vermilion border
thus transitioning the boundary
between dream time and no time (between
astral wilderness and human civilization).

I see multiple perspectives of myself,
both from above, and from below;
as a part of, and apart from.

I become light itself; I literally project
beam-like across the cosmic ocean. I am
transported within and through the cyberweb
of Indra's intertidal, iridescent, interpolatry net.

The Fine Structure Constant

I traverse the implicate enfoldment and return,
again and again, by way of the endlessly
circuitous explicate unfoldment.

One becomes two; two becomes many; the particulate
become wave-like. The wholestalt condenses and
coalesces, and transposes the refrain to yet another
variation of the dancing/singing measureless amplitude.

One pierces the veil and communicates directly,
diaphonically and thus intuitively with the
core lifetronic essence.

One matures, evolves, graduates and earns the
privilege of non-return. One becomes synoptic,
sequentially pleromatic, and fully and magnanimously
ontotheoic.

The self expands into *geist spume,* and glides
calmly and joyously in
lightless light,
darkless dark, and
thoughtless thought.

One glides forever, ineffable, ever-existent;
as the butterfly of omnipresence, on wings
etched with stars, moons and suns.

Keith Whittingslow

Intoxicated with ecstasy and bliss
in the One's dream of infinite, soaring
effortless/beingful flight …

Ergo

One glides … one is.

Sic itur ad astra.

Prism

Proust's mystery: that the essence of an immediate experience is a mirage, and that only in retrospect can its fullness be realized; a perspective whereby even scandalously painful episodes are seen afresh as no longer injurious. Proust was seemingly aware of the master template from which any and all events are composed, and thus of the totality with which they are constituted, as opposed to *just* subjectively feeling *only* the good or the evil of the present moment — of which he was prevalently and all too painfully conscious. By envisioning events magnanimously as frameless aspects of suspended eternity in which *telos* and *initio* are coterminous, he thus actualized that cool objectivity which is not the coldness of indifference, but rather the benevolent passivity of Tao observing Tao.

Recherché (thinking, experiencing, writing) is not then simply a self-reflexive, random, authorless, processual mind-game, rather it is a rich, complex, *prescriptive* which dissolves imperfections, melts down impurities, and translates raw experience into unique substantive essences. The recherché not only dissolves boundaries, but provides a sense of harmony and union, letting all things inexorably flow; as opposed to textual dissection, which exposes the fractures (and tears) of deconstruction.

Interpretation and perspective are (very close to being) everything.

Schopenhauer's *distancing* of representations subdues the quasi-subjective conscious *will* allowing us to apprehend the purely objective inner nature of events — and the pristine *ideas* inherent in them. The difficulty we have in implementing this process lies in our limited ability to intellectually subdue and/or eliminate the seemingly substantive conscious *will*. Said another way, in the immediate perception of the world, and of life, we consider things as a rule merely in their relations, and consequently according to their relative, not their absolute, essence. Yet, if we can experience a momentary enhancement of the intensity of our intuitive intelligence, we can at once see things with entirely different eyes; we can apprehend events no longer according to their relations, but according to what they are in and by themselves. Thus, in addition to relative existence we suddenly perceive absolute existence as well. As Goethe says:

> What in life does us annoy,
> we in picture do enjoy.

Memory is omnipotent — but it can kill as well as cure. Mnemonic virtuosity is the key to omniscience. Mirrored self-reflections (during morning ablutions for example) evoke a bizarre sense of reinterpretation of past (both near and distant) representations. Occurrences which I *know* were distasteful, suddenly reappear as happy remembrances. I equivocate — but enter once more into the experience. I practice once again the re-cognitive (to know it anew) recherché. I become a prism as I reposition my being in order to spectrally manifest, effulgent, untold and heretofore unimagined combinations of becoming. A prism can either capture (subdue/retain) and distort light, or it can send forth pleromatic bursts and blossoms of newly constituted diadems with ever-unique sheens, arrays and hues. It is the prism's responsibility to engender its own orientation. I posit once more that poets are the trustees of the magical aspects of memory. They keep and protect the metaphors of human experience. The work of the poet is to expose and uphold that which is universally transcendent and to allow it to *radiate*

The Fine Structure Constant

through *particularity.* Mindfulness generates becoming, allowing it to fold back into and then out of itself — the *poem* thus engenders and assures the ubiquitous and uroboric *eternal recurrence.*

Progressions

Toward Light, Revelation and Communion

A	alpha	asymptos	apocalypse
B	bathys	being	beth'el
Γ	golem	gamos	gnomon
Δ	daimon	dasein	dominion
E	evil	existentialism	enlightenment
Z	zelos	Zoroaster	Zion
H	haides	hagios	heofon
Θ	theodicy	thaumatos	theophania
I	erebus	eironeia	erasthai
K	kenosis	kabbala	kismet
Λ	logos	leitmotif	light
M	mythos	myein	metempsychosis
N	natus	nexus	nous
Ξ	xenos	xanthippe	xp
O	onta	orexis	om
Π	perdito	purgatorio	paradiso
P	rudis	ratio	rhodon
Σ	sin	siddhi	Shekhinah
T	tamas	tattva	Tao
Y	upadhi	upasana	utopia
Φ	physis	philos	photismos
Ξ	ch'i	chi'ng	Christos
Ψ	psilos	psalmos	psyche
Ω	osmos	omniscience	omega

Vak

SymPhonics of the Soul

Brahman, the creator, remains in a profound state of trance. He is silence, stillness. A thought, however, anticipates movement within. It manifests itself as song; the goddess Vak becomes the universe itself as energy. Of that energy all subenergies are born. Vak in Indo-European/Proto-Sanskrit philology is the same as the Latin *vox* and the English *voice*. The goddess takes on another name: she is also called *Sarasvati*, which means 'the flowing one' and she is recognized in India as the goddess of poetry, music and learning.

Modern physics, in brief format, posits: Energy flows steadily from suns (stars) throughout the universe. In earthly/worldly terms energy flow organizes matter into increasingly ordered states. A seeming *equipoise* ensues involving the ceaseless clustering of bonded atoms into molecules of higher and higher complexity along with the emergence of cycles for the storage and release of energy. Thus, a nonequilibrium steady state becomes likely in which energy would not just flow to the earth and radiate away. It would become, then, quantum-mechanically inevitable that it must rearrange matter into symmetry, away from probability, against entropy, and transliminally (so to speak) enhancing and augmenting it into a constantly changing condition of rearrangement of molecular ornamentation. This process, in terms of dynamic resonance, might have the structure of a Beethoven's Ode to Joy, or the instinctive elemental singing, and the rhythmic chanting chorus and pulse of all sentient creatures — whether they be insects, birds, whales, and/or humans. (It is said in Sanskrit poetics that the original poetry is the sound of running water, and the wind in the trees.)

A certain porcupine of our acquaintance reflects on this universal *fundamentum* by way of the following elucidation: The phenomenal world (nature) and music are two different expressions of the same *thing*. This *thing* is the *medium* of the analogy, and a thorough knowledge of it necessary in order to understand said analogy. Music, as an expression of the world is in the highest degree a universal language (and as such is also inseparable from concepts [universals] which in turn are inextricable from contexts [particulars]. Its universality is not abstract, but is united with both thoroughness and distinctive definitiveness. As such it resembles geometric figures and numbers (universal forms of all things) and is applicable to them *a priori*. All willful doing, (reason *and* feeling) may be expressed by the infinite number of possible melodies, but always in universal, metaphysical, and non-phenomenalistic expressions.

This profound relation of music to the true nature of all things explains why suitable music discloses the secret meaning to any event, and is the most accurate and distinct commentator on, and of, it. Immersion in the impressions of a symphony causes one to see all life/ world events taking place within him/herself. Music is distinguished from all other art forms, then, in that it is not a copy of, but is the *thing in itself*. But, the *analogy* recognized by the composer between universal and particulars, must somehow proceed from a *direct* knowledge of nature, unknown by reason. It must not be intentionally and conceptually produced by *contextual* means. Otherwise the music will not express inner nature, but merely an inadequate imitation of the phenomena. Thus, music is understood as the immediate language of the soul; and we feel our being stimulated to give form to this invisible and yet so actively stirred spirit world which speaks to us; and we feel prompted to embody it in an *analogous* example.

With respect to the above insights, we humble students of The Glass Bead Game here at Castalia, can only nod in admiration and ascent. Though we aspire to be able to understand and thus engage in the production of poetry, music, and song with the power and precision of the masters, we at this stage admit that we are still groping our way within, and hopefully through, the seemingly empty *pitaka* of abyss. We take heart, though, that the irony of our struggle, as it is the essential condition of responsible art and being, may yet prove to be the catalyst leading to the fullest aesthetic expression of *Das Glasperlenspiel*. Music, then, in all of its enthralling and *SymPhonic* aspects, may ultimately be the vehicle that leads us out of the remote human regions from which we derive; its flow representing the bright filaments and threads spun through the corridors of the labyrinth helping us to find a way out into the open.

Journeying

Is there an ein sof, a vast continuum, a beginning without end? Do Eckhart's *Nichts*, John of the Cross's *nada*, the Taoist *wu*, the Buddhist *sunyata*, and the Hindu *svatantra* express identical, vaguely similar, or totally disparate meanings?

Devolution

The Dark Wood. *The spiraling, silvery, glistening, opaque ill-defined longings manifest as* corpus loci *of desire within, spark the dark red urge-soaked deep burning embers of want, and awaken to peer enviously and jealously through eager green-gold eyes to further covet the forbidden essences in the image warped unplumbed ignorant depths of the reflecting pool of hyle, and are thus drawn, time-out-of-mind, into and through the deadly force-field of quasi attractiveness. The humanmoth is drawn into the flame.*

~~~~~~~

Is the *sefirot*, with its dimensions and developments of *ayin*, congruent in terms of meaning with the allegorical notions of *La Divina Commedia*? Are all souls *palimpsestual* and *pentimentic*, in that they record, over and over again, the words, images, and *qualia* of life's experiences? Does the soul repent, renew, transform and develop to a final, true and perfected format? Is there *suchness*, with variations and transformations - simply differing dimensions and perspectives

- of the *all*? Or, is there an *other,* with defined loci, such as the ice-centered cavern within the *inferno,* the middle ground and pathway up and around the mountain of *purgatorio,* thus leading to a final and absolute *paradiso*? Does *Tat Tvam asi* - That thou art - imply an *ein sof,* or does wakefulness and searching lead inexorably to a Kingdom? Is there a kingdom on earth? Is there a *different* kingdom in heaven?

Evolution

The Mountain. *The self enters, through the mirrored looking glass, into the vast hypnotic and entrancing reflections of all and everything. Along the endless experiential hallways and corridors of being, psychotropically and psychedelically engrossed; stoked, flushed, dancing, soaring, and blindly drawn to the beckoning yet still dim glimmer of light. Rushing wildly (though increasingly more mindful) through switchbacks, mazes, serpentines and into all of the dark hidden corners of the house-of-many-mansions. Finally, sensing a greater purpose, the semi-crystallized ego begins to discern a pattern, a rhythm, and a potential apocalypse. The faint stirrings of revelation transmute from heretofore uncontrolled inertia to a more definitive* modus vivendi operandi. *The self, sensing a larger Self, advances, as yet inexplicably, from existing, through becoming, toward Being.*

~~~~~~~

Does the soul, then, journey, and thus change? Or, does it more accurately remember, recognize, (know again), actualize, and realize its true nature? Is there a difference? Or, by posing the question are some of us unnecessarily splitting interpretive (and humanly uninterpretable) hairs? Is there a real immersion, from *pleroma,* into the *amnios,* through the *placenta,* into all of the seeming titillation's, tribulations and terrors of worldly/earthly realms? Is there a way out, a release from the chains, and off the wheel, finally and for good, and into nirvana, moksha, heaven and paradise. Or is Atman really Brahman, and samsara really nirvana?

Revolution

The White Rose. *Blinding white brilliance of purity itself. Energy, thought, being, doing, all as attributes, aspects and variations of the energy that is eternal delight. Transliminal, transtemporal, transhuman, transbeing. Truth. Freedom. God beyond God. The transtheistic power symbolizing the fullness of being that transcends being itself.* Ayin - *the mysterious palace in which everything dwells.*

~~~~~~~

Recapitulation: Is there a soul, and what is its true nature? Perhaps there is, but it is not knowable by means of prevalent conventional discriminative knowledge. However, discriminative knowledge as a form of consciousness, may well be the only vehicle by which liberations are attained; and thus conscious knowledge (wisdom?) might paradoxically reveal the fact that consciousness can never be bound.

Human perception of things masks their true nature - humanus semenza menzogna. *All may have been (or may be) undifferentiated in the depths of a great void. Yet, like ink concealed in a well, thought becomes manifest through the power of the writer, who draws it forth with his pen, and draws the writing as he wishes.*

AYIN * SamkhyaYoga * Tao * Nichts * Nada * Wu * Sunyata * Heaven * ALEF

Essence and Substance

Form: Interpolated variously both as explications/extensions, and implicate/impressions of content. Content: Endless variations, reflections, and interpretations of formatted (discrete) and non-formatted (raw/typal) form.

Taken together form and content can be experienced symbolically as renditional variants of Indra's universal net whereby the universe is considered to be a vast web of many-sided and highly polished jewels, each one acting as a multiple mirror. In one sense each jewel is a single entity. But when we look at a jewel, we see nothing but the reflections of other jewels, which themselves are reflections of other jewels, and so on in an endless system of mirroring. Thus in each jewel is the image of the entire net. Some manifestations of the net, seen as form, content, substance and process are:

Heart: The core constituent of *Sorge* (German - concern, caring) and, according to Heidegger, the essential structure of consciousness and the world.; the basis of all *being*.

Mind/Soul: Interface (event-horizon) of biological/physiological and metaphysical process. A blending of neuroelectrochemical (mind/brain) and non-particulate, wave-like pure intentionaloid thought.

Keith Whittingslow

Will: Both of the objective, and subjective variety. Taken together as *the* elemental projective motivational (bootstrapping) force. Subtle and nuanced at times engendering pure direct and benevolent seeing; yet capable of brute, blind, emotional and destructive rampage.

Partial grouping of both controlled, and random uncontrolled effects/affects (representations) of the essential and substantive web/net (jewel-like) manifestations (reflections): Rapier and bludgeon; glint and flint; (the obverse of *concern* is *angst*.) Ice-blue cold hermeneutic (doubt) and cerulean pastoral acceptance (belief). *Sturm* and *drang;* sweetness and light.

Golden motes (hope); molten irony; mindless luciferous blood-red desire.Gestaltic synaptic/synopsis: The hint and glint of ice-blue hermeneutical rapiers and bludgeons internally illuminate placid green mists, and sentient pearl-blue-grey sheens and matrices of joy, while at the same time issuing forth the finely and delicately knurled but wrath-like limns, emanations and anxiety-laden dark metallic adumbrations of angst. Simultaneously suspended (hopeful) golden motes coexist alongside presuppositional cerulean belief systems; both are buffeted, in one direction by reddish uncontrollable (belief-laden) arrhythmic blood feuds, and in the other direction by cold blue known accepted (belief-laden) pastoral symbioses.

Remedy (Latin - re + *medialis,* return to the middle, a cure, a correction).

Enter fully, but knowingly (suspended belief) into the center of the *cirque*. Examine, return, construct (and deconstruct so as to be able to reconstruct endlessly) ever-new models of all realities, conditions, perspectives and interpretations. Resist free-flowing, as well as, stagnant waters. Touch bottom frequently to test groundedness and position.

The Fine Structure Constant

Think of the universe as a pearl which is not of a single hue, but whose *essence* and *substance* are composed of interstitially incandescent, red-blue-fire-suffused opalescent *chakras*.

Imagination + tincture of *irony* (speech dissemblers) = Essence and Substance.

Driven

Elaunein, employed in the original Greek sense;
to drive elation, to lift up, exalt, and elevate the spirits.

Exquisite *elytrons* roll round cocoon-like, providing protective cover;
at the same time generating *aufgehoben,* as per Hegel (lift and preservation).

Elegant emerald egesta emanate, in their return cycle,
from *Elysian* fields enroute, again, for the billionth time, to *Arcadia.*

Euphe*mystic* elevation - or elemental elegiacal ephemera?

Am I the driver, or the driven? Am I the *ampersand?* Do I travel alone through amethyst constellations, or am I one with trembling golden meadows, seething subterranean serpents, and shimmering vivid green mountains? Are *seething* and *shimmering,* just two aspectical perspectives of one and the same phenomena?

Is to ask, to begin to know? Is knowledge preparatory to wisdom? Does wisdom mean acceptance? Is there light in air, intention in thought; ideas, imagination and meaning in the *akashic* ether? Is there a substance in the void? Is there blissful ignorance, or simply vast gaps in our understanding of the *paranatural?*

The Fine Structure Constant

For now, I push and pull; yield, and forge; drive, and am driven. Tomorrow (to the extent that time exists in formats other than those which are, paradoxically and eternally, *now*) I will dance to the refrain that I compose, and by which I am existentially (and sometimes even ecstatically) by choice, carried away.

Passages

The surging, oceanic, intertidal, infinite/unbound,
yet incrementally deep fissures of

$$time <\text{---------}> emit$$

a fluvial process whereby specious space
unfolds constantly into ever-event-filled horizons.

Light enters the clear lens of the eye
while pulsing fuse-like between
radiating nodal force-field matrices.

Sound reverberates vertiginously,
carrying all-that-is from nowhere to
everywhere, and back again.

Thought transforms no-thing into
every-thing.

Song emanates from silence.

Pleroma and void are one.

Truth relies on method.

The Fine Structure Constant

Purpose requires intent.

Poetry is the true science *(Novalis)* and is the sole arbiter of actuality.

To transcend the ground-of-all-being is a contradiction in terms. Hence transformation, ironically, and mysteriously, remains a process forever mythically, symbolically and metaphorically dependent.

To kill *time* is to *emit* dharmic dereliction.

Openings and Transitions

Heidegger speaks of the *eukukleos Aletheie,* well rounded unconcealment itself, as the possible opening. And he asks "is the task of thinking, then, not Being and Time, but Opening and Presence? But where does the opening come from, and how is it given? What speaks in the 'there is, it gives'; and is the task of thinking, then, the surrender of previous thinking to the determination of the matter *(sache)* for thinking?" He also talks of two fundamental modes of existing in the world: a state of forgetfulness of being (inauthentic - nonbeing) and a state of mindfulness of being (authentic - ontologic).

Borges posits that "universal history may be the history of the different intonations given a handful of metaphors". He traces the Sphere metaphor at least back to Xenophanes (6th century BCE) and says that many variations of the absolute can be distilled down to "Nature (God) is an intelligible sphere whose center is everywhere and whose circumference is nowhere". He also talks about the Mirror of Enigmas in describing the symbolic value of the world's sacred scriptures, and quotes De Quincy "Even the articulate or brutal sounds of the globe must be all so many languages and ciphers that somewhere have their corresponding keys - have their own grammar and syntax; and thus the least things in the universe must be secret mirrors to the greatest".

The Chinese pictogram which represents the notion of "crisis", is made up of two primary characters, danger and opportunity.

The Fine Structure Constant

Novalis wrote that "The greatest magician would be the one who would cast over himself a spell so complete that he would take his own phantasmagorias as autonomous appearances. Would not this be the case?" Borges conjectures that it is so. "We (the undivided divinity operating within us) have dreamt the world. We have dreamt it as firm, mysterious, visible, ubiquitous in space and durable in time; but in its architecture we have allowed tenuous and eternal crevices of unreason which tell us it is false".

As for myself, I continue to transit the many worlds while interpolating all signs, leitmotifs and mandalas. I walk all paths breathlessly, from moment to moment, interpreting reflexive glyphs, mantras and metaphors. I consider all conceivable alternatives and possibilities. I press on, finding temporary intellectual and intuitive solace in oriental pictograms, mindful modes, and enigmatic mirrors. I simultaneously fuel and check imaginative analyses with a self-concocted bittersweet elixir composed of *colloid* of care, *suspension* of judgment, *tincture* of time, and *essence* of sorgeaic skepticism. The primary questions dealing with meaning and purpose remain unanswered. But perhaps by extending the thrall and living the spell, while invoking gnoseal skepticism, I will somehow experience a fullness of spirit as it knowingly and consciously transits my eternally open window-of-being. A window which has no frames, yet willfully radiates auras (event-horizons) of intentionality, perseverance and hope.

Relation and Reciprocity

Ideas splash over my field of view;
I contemplate the world in and through a flood of light.
Texture and timbre permeate my senses.
The spectacle is manifold.
There are phases, poles,
aspects and dimensions.

In one sense I am dissolved,
immersed, and embedded,
in a field of expression.
I feel motion, pulse and presence.
Through grace I am seized, absorbed and drawn in.
I accept.

In another sense I bracket, frame and name
the whirlwind.
I understand the forces and elements as functions and processes
which continually adjust according to fixed and known canon.
I know the formulae and thus I arrange,
direct and control.
I assign.

But it can happen that providence and will, combine,
to form another unique expression.

The Fine Structure Constant

Object and subject are inextricably fused.
I encounter a pure reciprocal relationship.
Being both breathes, and is breathed.

The recurrent firmament defies description.
We are motes, and thus quanta in the vast space-time grid.
Yet we are also one and the same as the indissoluble matrix.

Relationship is more than it can ever know.
Ineluctably I make, but am beyond comprehension, made.
Interpretation here falls short;
here is the fount of all actual life.

The droplet and the ocean are reciprocally one.
Images wash through the viewer's mind.

All life is encounter.

All relationship is reciprocal.

Dasein and Ayin

Sartre

Being *(être)*. Being is. Being is in-itself. Being is what it is. Being includes both Being-in-itself and Being-for-itself, but the latter is the nihilation of the former. As contrasted with existence, Being is all-embracing and objective, rather than individual and subjective.

Heidegger

Something like 'Being' has been disclosed in the understanding-of-Being which belongs to existent Dasein as a way in which it understands. Being has been disclosed in a preliminary way, though non-conceptually; and this makes it possible for Dasein as existent Being-in-the-world to comport itself *towards entities* - towards those which it encounters within-the-world as well as towards itself as existent.

Kabbalah

'Being is in nothingness ... The effect is in the cause after the mode of the cause, and the cause is in the effect after the mode of the effect' (*Liber de Causis* - anonymous Neoplatonic; and Moses de Leon [thirteenth century] *Sheqel ha Qodesh*).

The Fine Structure Constant

Sartre

Being-for-itself (être-pour-soi). The nihilation of Being-in-itself; Consciousness conceived as a lack of Being, a desire for Being, a relation to Being. By bringing Nothingness into the world the For-itself can stand out from Being and judge other beings by knowing what it is not. Each For-itself is the nihilation of a particular being.

Heidegger

How is this disclosive understanding of Being at all possible for Dasein? Can this question be answered by going back to the *primordial constitution-of-Being* of that Dasein of which Being is understood? The existential-ontological constitution of Dasein's totality is grounded in temporality.

Kabbalah

'Wisdom comes into being out of ayin' Job 28:12, usually translated: 'Where is wisdom to be found?' But the Hebrew word ayin can mean 'nothing' as well as 'where', and various thirteenth-century kabbalists employ this alternate meaning. Job's rhetorical question is thereby transformed into a mystical formula: 'Divine wisdom comes into being out of nothingness.'

Sartre

Being-in-itself *(être-en-soi).* Non-conscious Being. It is the Being of the phenomenon and overflows the knowledge which we have of it. It is a plenitude, and strictly speaking we can say of it only that it is.

Heidegger

The ecstatical projection of Being must be made possible by some primordial way in which ecstatical temporality temporalizes.

Kabbalah

The concept of the ether (Hebrew, *avir,* air) corresponds to Greek conception. Aristotle identified ether as an incorruptible, unchangeable element, rotating among the spheres, filling all of space. The Stoics identified the ether with *pneuma,* a quasi-material spiritual substance which pervades all space and matter, as well as transmitting light and gravity. Descartes' 'subtle matter' corresponds to the ether, as does the active vacuum field in contemporary particle physics. In classical Kabbalah the ether is identical with the highest sefirah, also as nothingness (ayin) - the creative nothingness out of which all being emerges.

Sartre

Being-for-others *(être-pour-autrui).* The third ekstasis of the For-itself. There arises here a new dimension of being in which my Self exists outside as an object for others. The For-others involves a perpetual conflict as each For-itself seeks to recover its own Being by directly or indirectly making an object out of the other.

Heidegger

How is this mode of the temporalizing of temporality to be interpreted? Is there a way which leads from primordial *time* to the meaning of *Being?* Does *time* itself manifest itself as the horizon of *Being?*

The Fine Structure Constant

Kabbalah

Ayin symbolizes the fullness of being that transcends being itself, 'the mysterious palace of *ayin*, in which everything dwells'. The appearance of things belies their origin; 'all was undifferentiated in the depths of ayin'. The reality that animates and surpasses all things cannot be captured or named, but by invoking *ayin* the seeker is able to allude to the infinite, to *alef* the ineffable.

Ich bin ein dichter

Words flow.

Thesis, antithesis, synthesis;
in the beginning was the word;
in the middle there were/are more words.

In the end? There may not be an end ... and in actuality probably not a beginning ... just the eternal *flow* (becoming) ... of words, variously interpreted as *being, nothingness, time* and *space* ... but always measureless, recursive and quasi-interpretable.

Ein dichter is a dialectician;
ein dichter makes words ... and in turn, words make *ein dichter*;
ein dichter interprets ... and is quasi-interpretable

Words flow.

Nexus

Void

pure mind, will, conscience (omniscience) gnosis, pure energy

Ein Sof

electro magnetic energy

withdrawal

light

falls into

firmament

tsimtsum

shevirah

tiqqun

℘

Matter

sub-atomic particles, atoms, molecules, combinatory milieu, inherent energy

The Fine Structure Constant

organization

℘

Plant

cellulose, parenchyma, photosynthesis, respiration, passive energy

typality

℘

Animal

protomind, semi-social, protoconscious, instinctual protoneural energy

archetypality

℘

Human

awakening mind, socially conscious, self-reflexive, meta-neural energy

ideologicality

℘

Planet

oceanic-atmospheric Gaia-consciousness, macro-mind, mega-neural energy metanoiality

℘

Galaxy

star-sun-planet-spirals, trans-neural systems, encodation/imprintation

pan psychality

℘

Cosmos

cosmic <-neural-> energy, expansion<-+->contraction, endless<-evernew->replique

alphaomegality

℘

Multiverse

elemental dust, cyber-gas, super-condensed-quasi-neural energy

chaos <—-> order

black holes <-+-> event<light>horizon <-+-> quasars

Blown out Satori   ∞   Withdrawn Nirvana

The Fine Structure Constant

Brahman/Ein Sof

℘

Ontogeny Recapitulates Phylogeny

Ontologicality

∞

Infinite Shekinah Self-Recapitulates Eternally

⇕

ayin

⇕

tsimtsum

⇕

shevirah

⇕

tiqqun

⇕

NEXUS

The Perfume River

If the question of meaning in life
is not edifying, as Buddha has said;
we can do as he suggests; that is,
immerse ourselves in the river of life
and let the question
drift away.

Or we can posit, with Ibsen,
that we are all dead;
and the Last Judgment will be
the day when we dead awaken.
It will be the moment when the first human being
struggles ashore from the vicious and seducing whirlpool
that makes us more animal than human.
In such a moment - envisioned by Blake and Nietzsche -
history will end, and real time begin.

Time is a river of the imagination;
memory fuels imagination.
Without memory, life is a barren desert;
a person without memory is an horizon-less event.

The Fine Structure Constant

The universe is real in proportion to the restriction
of memory and anticipation.
Memory is the instrument of human consciousness ...
and is the key to prehension.

Once, in another time, another place ... another dimension ...
I traveled daily the Perfume River, to and from The Imperial City.
At the time I did not see the import, nor the meaning of that travel.

On reflection, I struggled to assert by means of memory, allegory,
and consciousness; and glimpsed through the river mist the ultimate
definition of the ideal of life.

As one uses a glass mirror to see one's face,
one must use works of art (imaginative consciousness)
to see one's soul.

Traveling the rivers of time, of memory and of imagination,
can lead to salvation;
but the passage must be an actively conscious one.
If the journey is only a ride,
then Buddha's *anatta* is indeed a sterile realization.

Here it seems that the Buddha has been misunderstood;
or, he himself misunderstood.
His method - negative ontology,
was not meant to be an end - only a means.

Keith Whittingslow

Certainly the raft is dispensable upon reaching the far shore;
but it remains essential (one cannot cross the river without it)
if one is to even attempt the crossing at all.

There is an Imperial City.
The Perfume River does lead to it.
But one must actively choose (swim toward) enlightenment,
and not simply float along in calm (but stagnant) waters.

Abeam of Reality

I

Steinerian aspirants contemplate the notion that out of a small seed, enticed by the forces of earth and light, grow plants of complex structure. The seed thus contains something invisible enfolded within it, and, that which ultimately grows out, is in fact embedded within as the *force of the whole plant.* This seemingly invisible and non-existent something, then, is a *reality* which transmutes the invisible into the visible. My exegesis is that the 'something' is a *reality* which exists *side-by-side* with a seeming non-reality, and that it is one which can be actualized only by intensely *observing* the process and by *thinking* about the profundity of reality *as* simultaneity.

II

Scientifically-minded aspirants ponder the evolution of the cosmos, and wonder if space travel will enable us to transmute our theories into absolute knowledge and thus arrive at a final understanding of *all-that-is.* Well, it so happens, according to Gary Snyder, that we are already in space and have been traveling (on planet Earth) great distances at great speeds. So where is the *reality?* Does one need to go to the ends of the universe to find truth? Or, were Blake and Eliot particularly prescient in their descriptions of scale and cycle. Can the universe *really* be seen in a grain of sand?

Will we find that the end of all of our exploration will be to arrive where we started and know the place, realistically *and* simultaneously, for the first time?

III

Frank Oppenheimer said that the basis for social and technical change lies in our understanding of how nature behaves, and of how people behave. If humanity can achieve higher levels of understanding *reality*, then the *real* world will be significantly improved. To those who argued that we already live in the *real* world, Oppenheimer responded that it is not so - 'we live in the world we made up". Oppenheimer's legacy is the *Exploratorium*, which helps us to see, simultaneously, the elegance *and* unity in nature and *reality*.

IV

Buber said that the human entity is the 'crystallized potential of existence'. And, he concluded that the unique quality of being human is to be found not in the individual, nor in the collective, but in the I *and* Thou'. The I-Thou can be described as the dialogical 'in-between', the *relation* between things (*dazwischen* - there in-between). So, humanity is both finite and infinite; and is not good nor evil by nature, but rather is composed of *polarities*. Our essential problematic of the *between* is the duality of *being* and *seeming*, a question of calculated *image* versus pure spontaneous *imagelessness*. The *reality* of being, then, is a question of polar emphasis toward *authenticity* of being, as opposed to the construction of a *seeming* appearance of being.

The Fine Structure Constant

V

It seems that in the final analysis, the question of *what* one knows stands upon the question of *how* one knows. Thus, ontology is dependent upon epistemology - and the extension of this notion might mean that in order to understand and value *reality*, one would need to sense the articulate unity of both physics and metaphysics. Some philosophers are aware of the synonimity of certain terms, hence - *reality = ontology = metaphysics*. Balancing one's being in time and space, then, might require that one constantly be abeam of *reality* - in all of its manifestations, permutations, combinations and interpretations.

VI

There may be many ways that appear to align with reality. But, the indwelling navigator homes only along those frequencies which are truly and authentically *abeam* of reality.

Some Aspects of Circularity and Wholeness

The Hermeneutic Circle

Everything turns on the logic of implicit and explicit,
hence there is nothing vicious in a circular
phenomenological/hermeneutical logic.

Being and becoming is a work of unfolding, explicating,
laying out the implicit fore-structures
which make explicit experience possible.

Indeed, without continually unfolding horizons
no entity or object could ever appear.

A circular analytic proof is unavoidable
because such an analysis does not prove,
according to the rules of a logic of consistency;
hence the contingent, context-bound, provisional, and self-delimited logic
of Goedel, Heisenberg, and Wittgenstein, to name only a few.

Common sense may wish to eliminate circularity,
on the supposition that it is employing rigorous scientific investigation,
but it finds that circularity represents

The Fine Structure Constant

nothing less than the basic structure of caring.
(Caring is one pole of the hub - Sorge/Concern - Angst the other.)

The existential circle (the ontological loop) is derived
from a philosophy of repetition.
Hermeneutic circularity is thus a subsystem
of ontological circularity.
Hermeneutics cannot be understood in ontologically neutral terms.

Hermeneutics is a complex circulatory system in which the circles weave
and interweave to inscribe pattern and sense in being ...
the circle is at one and the same time the model for the ontology of being,
for the work of the understanding, and for the strategy of the text.
Hermeneutics is illusory because it eludes definite beginnings
and distinct conclusions.
It attempts to steer through the flux, but in the (human) end,
claims of conclusions are denied.
Hence, rather than closure, one should instead seek opening.
Ultimately, hermeneutics leaves us with the notion that there is,
in a mysterious sense, only the 'play within a play'.

We can question ad infinitum who it is that writes the plays,
and who might be the players?
But for now, it seems, all we realize is that ... the play is all.

Hermetic Wholeness

An ancient idea, Hermeticism - that finds at least some expression
in virtually all of the world's philosophical and metaphysical traditions -
comes full circle.

Keith Whittingslow

Hermes Trismegistus:
The without is like the within of things;
the small is like the large.

Empodocles:
God is a circle whose center is everywhere,
and whose circumference is nowhere.

Medieval Alchemy:
As above, so below.

Hindu Visvara Tantra:
What is here is elsewhere.

Sufism:
The macrocosm is the microcosm.

William Blake:
The world in a grain of sand.

Black Elk:
Anywhere is the center of the world.

Hindu Avatamsaka Sutra:
Each object in Indra's universal net is not only itself, but encompasses,
reflects, and involves every other object;
and indeed *is* everything else.

Fa-Tsang and Hua-Yen Buddhism:
A candle in a room full of mirrors represents the relationship
of the One to the many.

The Fine Structure Constant

A polished crystal in the center of the same room represents the relationship of the many to the One.

Kabbalah:
... entire creation is an illusory projection of the transcendental aspects of
(the deity) ... for every reflection of reality, even remote, broken up and transparent, necessarily possesses something of its cause.

Shamanism:
The central concept of shamanism, wherever in the world it is found, is the notion that
underlying all the visible forms in the world, animate and inanimate, there exists a vital
essence from which they emerge and by which they are nurtured. Ultimately everything
returns to this ineffable, mysterious, impersonal unknown.

Holography

Gottfried William Leibniz:
Developed the integral calculus. Studied Hua-Yen Buddhism. Proposed that the universe is constituted of fundamental entities ... monads, each of which contains a reflection of the whole universe.

Hermann von Helmholtz:
Showed that the ear is a frequency analyzer.

Jean B. J. Fourier
Developed a modified calculus enabling images to be converted into a language of wave forms - and back again.

George von Bekesy:
Used Fourier logic to demonstrate that skin is sensitive to frequency vibration, and posited that taste may involve frequency analysis.

Dennis Gabor:
Used Fourier mathematical transforms to formulate theories that enabled the development of the hologram.

R. and K. DeValois:
Discovered that the brain functions by way of Fourier transforms in the conversion and deconversion of wave forms.

Nikolai Bernstein:
Discovered that human physiological movement is encoded in the brain in the language of Fourier wave forms

Karl Pribram:
Developed the holographic theory of the brain, and that not just vision, language and memory, etc., but the entire brain and nervous system are indeed holograms.

David Bohm:
Asserts theories of non-locality. Extends quantum theory to holography. Describes 'wholeness and the implicate order'. Postulates the undivided wholeness of all things, to include the makeup of the universe in its entirety, only one implication of which is that - consciousness is just a more subtle form of matter. Prefers the term holomovement over hologram, as the universe is not static, but is dynamic and ever-active with incalculable enfoldings and unfoldings that moment by moment create the 'universe'.

Bohm and Pribram:
Our brains mathematically construct objective reality by interpreting frequencies that are ultimately projections from another dimension, a deeper

The Fine Structure Constant

order of existence that is beyond both space and time. The brain is a hologram enfolded in a holographic universe. And finally, not only does the brain construct objects, but we even construct time and space itself.

~~~~~~~

The Aborigines:
Understood infinity as 'dream-time'.

Aurobindo:
Says that we evolve from soul-state,
to soul-state,
and from illumination to illumination.

The Perennial Philosophy:
So coined by Leibniz, says that all of the
above is universal wisdom,
and has been understood by some throughout eternity.
Nonetheless, most of us are just beginning to awaken,
and to learn the rudiments
of higher-order knowledge.

~~~~~~~

We are just learning how to survive in infinity.
The Hermes > Hermeneutic > Holomovement
progression
provides clues to the puzzle.

~~~~~~~

Golden Elixir

One of the goals of
Taoist sages was to become
an *hsien*, an immortal, a being
who would live forever in a sensual,
very material paradise.
One of the ways to become an *hsien* was by
searching out, and drinking
an alchemical Golden Elixir.

Confucianism, while contesting *hsien*-like entities,
nevertheless accepts spirit and the notion of afterlife.

Early Hindu thought, in the Rig Veda,
assumes a unity between soul and body,
and a resurrection of a united body and soul
ultimately occurring in an earthly paradise.
In modern Hindu and Buddhist thought, the idea of reincarnation
is based on a strict dualism between body and soul.
(Scholarly debate continues with regard to whether or not Nirvana
corresponds to heaven; whether or not the concept of a soul
corresponds with
the notion of a series of successive states; whether or not the notion of God
(or no-God) translates across theological exegeses; and whether or not monism,
dualism, non-dualism or 'there is only one Brahman without a second', correctly

The Fine Structure Constant

describes being and/or ultra-being.) Nonetheless, whether in the puranas, Advaita Vedantism, or in Theravada, Mahayana or Zen Buddhism, an eternal and/or immortal concept (whether earthly or heavenly) along with an actualization or realization process, prevails.

Abrahamic (Judeo-Christian-Islamic) traditions, generally speaking, assert that there is a personal God who created the universe and who, while imposing certain trials and contingencies, nonetheless ensures us that we will live in happiness after death; to wit, and afterlife does exist and it is attainable.

Recently, Frank Tipler usurped (he would say extended or augmented) Teilhard de Chardin's Omega Point Theory. According to Tipler, theology is now a branch of physics, and indeed the proof for the existence of God is now a 'beautiful pure physics construct'. The God hypothesis becomes modernized and absorbs theology into physics, to make heaven as real as an electron. Using the most advanced sophisticated methods of modern physics and relying solely on the rigorous procedures of logic that science demands, Tipler creates a proof of the existence of God - and posits that every human being who ever lived will be resurrected from the dead. God and resurrected beings will not be *Homo sapiens* though - but shall be intelligent machines, emulated as computers of the future. So, in this model, 'the physics of immortality', theology becomes a branch of physics, and God and salvation occur as per other theologies, except that in order to evolve to the Omega Point, which is neither space nor time nor matter and is not bio-physically possible, we transubstantiate not to a vague 'intelligent energy' as per prior scientific deistic generalizations, but as per the Many-Worlds Interpretation of cosmology, to become sophisticated quantum mechanical (but God-like) physical objects.

Keith Whittingslow

Some scientists, philosophers and poets (among whose ranks I count myself as at least a partial subscriber) see the importance of consciousness (to include knowing versus believing) as a discipline/pursuit which might possibly lead one to the equivalent of enlightenment and/or salvation. Indeed, a (unified) field theory of consciousness is described by Peter Koestenbaum as follows: being exists as polarities (mind/body, individual-universal, etc.); being is dialectical and its existence is dynamic and becoming either as life, with increasing foci and concentrations of energy through the evolution of species or individuals, or as entropy, with inert matter and decreasing foci of energy and increased evenness of energy distribution; life and entropy can be described as occurring on the model of a field (as in a magnet or a capacitor) which includes both stress and oscillation (which characterizes kinetic energy and wave phenomena); being, then is process rather than stasis, and a field theory of being as consciousness attempts to assess the significance of these conditions. The strength of field theory (phenomenology as dialectical philosophy) lies in the insight that 'evidence of unprejudiced and immediate experience discloses the irreducible fundamentum of reality to be a consciousness-object, subject-object, awareness-world continuum'. The polar continuities are co-constituted by their permanent interpenetration and interdependence. Consciousness and world or mind and matter are thus in direct touch with each other, and are part of one field. The problem of mind-matter interaction does not arise, because it is precisely this interaction that is given in the irreducible immediacy of presuppositionless experience. The basic idea is that intellectual process (philosophy), spiritual process (God-truth), and personal-social process (self-world realization/evolution), differ as process only in degree (quantitatively) and not in kind (qualitatively) and thus are seen to be spectrae of a continuum - and as such are knowable and accessible through the fields of phenomenology. Finally, it is suggested that phenomenology as field theory might represent an ever-new open-ended, dynamic,

The Fine Structure Constant

responsible and integrative way of combining scientific method,
subjective process, and spirituality.

~~~~~~~

In view of the above, and as I ponder the many systems,
(and being as I am an aspiring and somewhat conscious evolute)
rather obvious questions of mode, method and practice present themselves.

What's a body to do?

Well, first of all I sit at my trusty word crunching computer and imagine
myself melding, holographically, with the mysterious solid-state electronic
webwork that makes up the CPU of this electronic *logoic* synthesizer,
thus attempting to become a new and evolving bridge state of
virtual bio-transducer reality.

At the same time I gaze out of the window, expansively,
and imagine myself being one with the sublime continuum of beingness
as it expresses itself as a vast field of nature-consciousness.

Then I remember to audibly repeat my personal mantra,
thus invoking and realizing the golden Aum/Omega Point gestalt
which is consonant with the universal Gaia-cosmic energy state.

As a visual mandala I reflect on the sun-fused
liquid golden motes evanescing in my root beer, and on the
burnished golden glints winking out from within
the matrix of my corn chips.

But, in the final analysis, for me,

Keith Whittingslow

(aside from science, technology and religion; and in view of the
mysterium, both *fascinans* and *tremendum,* which are life, death and projections
of otherworlds and afterlifes) it is the golden alchemical elixirs of philosophy
and poetry that best evoke a quasi-transcendent state connecting
mundane ontological tangibility with
ethereal metaphysical spirit.

Twilight

Carlos Castaneda has Don Juan saying that . . .
. . . 'twilight represents the crack between worlds'.
Here, I concur, and simply add that when journeying
to Ixtlan one would do well to recall old Bach's suggestion;
Quaerendo invenietis.

Wagner's megalomaniacal leitmotifs, especially in Twilight of the Gods,
Gotterdammerung,
ultimately fail, (despite his Ragnarokian deceptions and diversions)
as do all attempts to falsely bolster Christianity
(notwithstanding the notion that even so-called legitimate attempts
to bolster Christianity are inherently doomed due to the flaw inherent in
Christianity itself).
Thus I expose myself here, as being with regard to the above,
thoroughly Nietzschean.

Nietzsche's philosophizing with a hammer
is not as is commonly thought, to employ
a sledge hammer.
On the contrary, a much more nuanced procedure takes place,
in his Twilight of the Idols
Gotzen-Dammerung,
which is the touching of all idols with a delicate tuning fork
in order to uncover inherent flaws.

Keith Whittingslow

Twilight is sunlight scattered once or (the fainter)
twice (AS *twi*-Two + *leoht* Light) hence a faint light
or obscure medium through which anything is viewed.
Everything is subject, thus, to dual-lit representations,
at dusk *and* dawn.

Ponder well, then, the transition between these two lights,
wherein are found all worlds, realms, dimensions and universes.
Interstellar space is bathed in eternal twilight,
the isologous holographic epiphaniacal interstitial *lux;*
the totality of the starlit whole.

Hegel counsels thus …
'The owl of Minerva spreads its wings
only with the falling of dusk'.

Suspense

Pyrrhic Reflections Beneath A Linden Tree

The empiricist presumes that sense perceptions
are given to our minds in their naked reality,
and that they are the basis of all knowledge.

To believe that we have access to language behavior
as a realm of fact or reality is surely to leap over
the first of all philosophical questions.

Human predicament is not resolved primarily through knowledge,
but by taking certain decisions about the nature of human well-being.
This is more a matter of a discipline of thought,
and of appropriate attitudes than it is a knowledge *about* things.

Suspension of judgment as principle
is more than a theory about the impossibility of knowledge,
it is a life attitude,
and so has implication for human well-being.

Keith Whittingslow

The unaware telos, the natural fulfillment -
not, the calculated reward - of suspension of judgment,
is serenity of mind.

Yet the attempts to completely suspend all judgment fail,
because we are unable to surrender the comfort of knowledge totally.

Knowledge by itself, cannot lead to well-being.
Knowledge, in itself, is indifferent to well-being.
The task of future thought will hinge on the question
concerning the human need to make sense out of life,
fulfilled in the absence of the certainty which knowledge gives us.

Eastern pronouncements that
'Knowing things is not the best way of being with things'
and 'Truth is not the concern of knowledge but of a life discipline'
echo back in rich discord from the oldest of reflective thought:
Knowledge being impossible, suspension of judgment bears its natural fruit
in untroubledness of soul,
the highest well-being of which humans are capable.

The idea-words *dream, magic,* and *source* claim preference to *knowledge,*
reality and *truth* in that, unlike these, they do not fail to fulfill
themselves when put to the vivial/life test.
Whereas *knowledge, reality* and *truth* abandon the thinker at the very point
where their promise should be kept, dissipating themselves
in their failed fulfillment;
dream, magic, and *truthing* evoke expectations which can be fulfilled.

The Fine Structure Constant

The more one is open to the fullness of vivial exploration,
to the many wondrous ways of making sense,
the more these ideas grow in strength.

Life ceases to bewilder as dream and magic
when one lives these ideas to their fulfillment.
So it can then be said,
paradoxically,
that human existence makes best sense as the not-sense
of magic and dream

Yet,
the profound dialogical holodynamic
lies in the reciprocal penetration
of knowledge *and* behavior,
each receiving its sense
from the other.

Meanwhile (and suspended just above, but polar-dimensions removed),
the Linden Tree thought,
'There are more bonds between the everyday and its source
than vivial thought and reflection;
but for now it is enough if the thinker is able to live out
what has been discovered thus far'.

Methodology
Provisionality And The Tertium Quid

Via Positiva:
Essentially - to believe. Methodologically misleading,
error-prone and inherently flawed.
Hard-wired, rose-colored-lens-filtered; happy-speak.
Contextualized.
Onto(theo)illogical.
Intolerable.

Via Negativa:
Essentially - to disbelieve. Guilty of category error,
premature closure and pre-trans (fallacy) confusion.
Legitimate but inauthentic; structure/stage misoriented.
De(con)textualized.
Onto(theo)nihilogical.
Dysfunctional.

Via Speculativa:
Essentially - Latin *observation* and *contemplation*. Another (third) way.
Relies on deduction rather than induction; assessment rather than
assignment.

The Fine Structure Constant

Holocontextualized.
Non-paradigmatic, presuppositionless; suspends judgment.
Ontological.
Life-embracing.

~~~~~~~

Provisionality:
Rigor, care, integrity.

Courage - to attack one's convictions!

To not apply
a method
... is itself a method ...
of ignorance and denial.

Employ skepticism - Greek *think, speculate.*
... semantically stimulate the gyrelogical ...
... envision ...
... interpret ...

Communicate!

Zeal

Passion And Emulation

The reward of seeking
is enlightenment.
But, it is first required that
quantification and qualification
(by the seeker, of that which is sought)
occurs.

Western (uni-polar) ardor:
Attempts to control nature.
Epistemologic.
Objective.
Explicative.
Assertive.
Yang.

Eastern (bi-polar) ardor:
Attempts to experience nature.
Axiologic.
Subjective.
Implicative.
Inferential.
Yin.

The Fine Structure Constant

Universal (omni-polar) ardor:
Pleromatic Naturale.
Ontologic.
Projective.
Reflexive/Replicative.
Definitive.
Tao.

The cosmic and the telluric
may indeed be
interlocking systems,
but they are known as such
only to those who through zeal,
become cognizant by way of certain
consciously developed senses.

The universe may indeed be filled
with energy suffused white light,
and the wave-web of the aether may roll-on into infinity,
but these profound processes become evident
only to those passionate detectors whose antennae
are fully attuned to perceive, and thus emulate,
the all.

Soul's Locus

Whither the soul?

Is it corporeal, or non-corporeal?

Have body, and soul, equivalence with mind, and psyche?

It seems that the soul cannot be located *anywhere,*
(not any one specific place, that is).

Perhaps then, the soul is *everywhere.*
Which would be to say, by definition,
that the soul is in fact *boundless.*

Considering our exploration of the aspect
of the soul relating to the body,
we might extrapolate that by everywhere corporeally,
we would mean that the soul is inseparable, and indistinguishable,
from every fiber, particle and drop of protoplasm
in the body.

Indeed, it would seem also that we *can* use mind, psyche and soul
interchangeably.
How else are we to describe the processes of vitality,
and optimality in our very being during times of

The Fine Structure Constant

peak sensuality?
(Putting aside for now those character-building experiences
such as solitude, and suffering.)

We must conclude, then, that those human experiences which
afford us the greatest freedom we can know,
result in and from the simultaneous liberation
of *both* body *and* mind.

Finally, in a certain (universal) sense, it appears
that the strength and power of the mind
are without limit.

Nonetheless, we are (most of us, for the most part)
at the moment, in the body.

Thus a prescriptive consisting of those time-honored techniques,
the mastering of which enhance life, energy and vitality,
will inevitably create psychoneuroontological vigor, optimality and richness.

ecce homo - body/soul synthesis - ecce psukhe

Subsets

Physics is a subset of biology.

Biology is a subset of anthropology.

Anthropology is a subset of sociology.

Sociology is a subset of psychology.

Psychology is a subset of philology.

Philology is a subset of theology.

Theology is a subset of cosmology.

Cosmology is a subset of *scienza*.

Scienza is a subset of art.

Art is a subset of poetry.

Poetry is a subset of axiology.

Axiology is a subset of epistemology.

The Fine Structure Constant

Epistemology is a subset of ontology.

Ontology is a subset of metaphysics.

Metaphysics is a subset of philosophy.

Philosophy is a subset of life.

Life is a subset of death.

Death is a subset of the fine structure constant.

The fine structure constant is a subset of universal consciousness.

Universal consciousness is a subset of the logos.

The logos,
as all else,
is simultaneously a subset, and the superset, of
itself.

II.

Jnanaic Senryu (Series)

Yes, I rest within
being's sea, blithely dancing
then, now, and nowhen.

The Fine Structure Constant

Restful Sea Ranch jaunt
just westward of Ukiah
haiku moods abound.

Waves break on beach
pencil, paper, ideas,
thoughts come flowing now.

Keith Whittingslow

Winding shoreline path
fungi, lichen and sagebrush,
primal tone-paintings.

Majestic stone cliffs
overlooking the vast sea,
nature's brood moves about.

The Fine Structure Constant

Fog, sky, ocean, sun,
an ethereal blending,
earth-sea horizons.

Warm sea breathing life
thoughts, feelings, doing - being,
spirit shining bright.

Keith Whittingslow

Dawn light emerges
bright, clear, resounding visions,
the source shines anew.

Morning sun rises,
vivid colors come to life,
sweet air breathes skyward.

The Fine Structure Constant

Exuberant space
awash with life-giving light
house of buoyant views.

Organic home
wood, glass, peacefully silent
the still-point is now.

Keith Whittingslow

Birds, darting, chirping,
dew sparkles on the lush grass,
wild meadow-land's morn.

Quasi ecstatique
we contemplate being's state
with sun, sand, and sea.

The Fine Structure Constant

Thematic critique
touching the essential pulse
central golden thread.

Strict dialectic
philosophical rigor
essential for truth.

Keith Whittingslow

Thought generates will,
actions test, express, confirm,
engender/create.

Time stands still in thought
doing engenders life's force
process is both/and.

The Fine Structure Constant

Yes ... we *are* the flux,
the ocean thinks, talks, feels, wills,
is philosophy.

Translucent dew drops
phase-dimensional rainbows
the great shining sea.

Keith Whittingslow

Christmas morn dawning
nature's critters start the day
flowers bathe in dew.

                                                  The backyard cat stalks
                                                  searches for a sunny glade
                                                  then bides - naps awhile.

Humans rush the day
chasing their tails all the while
critters watch the fray.

                                                  Life goes on for each
                                      'cept critters seem filed with grace
                                                      humans with dismay.

The Fine Structure Constant

Northernmost journey
polar horizon stillpoint
standing on the edge.

Motionless in space
suspended at its solstice
our star rests awhile.

A momentary end
time seemingly completed
yet, new paths beckon.

A crucial juncture
the pleroma's magnet pulls
life's dance continues.

Energy restored
vitality brimming full
souls shine resplendent.

Keith Whittingslow

A fresh beginning
projections of hope emerge
let us seek the light.

III.

Birthday Poems

L

A young raccoon
>in the hollow of a tree . . .

A meadow rabbit
>peeking to see . . .

The deer, the birds,
>all spying around . . .

What is it
>that stirs the ground . . . ?

Is it an earthquake,
>equinox, comet,
>or solstice . . . ?

Is it *fin de siecle,*
>the Armageddon,
>or harmonic convergence . . . ?

No, it's something
>much grander and bigger
>than nature's sway . . .

The Fine Structure Constant

It's Pat's blooming,
    joyous, and much deserved,
    splendidly gracious
    fiftieth birthday!

HURRAY . . . . *!!!*

Ephemeral Joy

Imagine . . . the simple, yet profound/divine joys
  of being in the quiet splendor of one's own garden.

Is this serene habitat a dimension of the ephemeral,
  yet seemingly transient, primal/cosmic dream-state?

Is it perhaps the *eternal* reality? Thus, are mundane/earthly,
  busy work-a-day, existential/experiential matters in
             actuality the surreal, ethereal, diaphanous,
                 illusory world of *Maya?*

Which is true?
                         Which is illusion?

Did Chuang Tze really awaken from a dream, in which he was a butterfly? Or, was he actually a butterfly, dreaming that he awoke human?

When and where does physical matter reality dissolve, disintegrate,
  disembody into metaphysical spirit?

The Fine Structure Constant

Where is the event-horizon, the boundary, the cross-over point*space, the transitional locus, the mind-body junctional interface?

Does it matter?

It depends upon one's interpretation and perspective, and we might do well to transport ourselves, more often, to the ephemeral and joyous garden,

For like all flowers, butterflies, people and ideas ... we constantly move through the cycle, the gyre, the rotation of beingness. Ever more reason, thus, to enhance all phases of experience by expanding our faculties of imagination and speculation.

Remembrance, the act of thought-event engenderance, evoking/invoking conceptual, perceptual, introceptual/extroceptual images ... may well be the key, the heart, the hinge, upon which all states and stages pivot.

Let us envision our sublime garden infused and suffused with imaginative, reflexive, ephemeral joyousness ... as we remember both the
implicative and explicative nodal points
of one of your
births.

North Coast Canticle

Earth's cadence sustains them - ethereal, tangible -
lush meadows and Monterey pines,
meandering trails,
forests that endure;

exuberant brooks pursue all paths,
capricious flowing pastoral harmony,
etching byways, streams of clarity
traversing mind's facades;

winds drift parabolically o'er idyllic palisades,
sculpting each moment with jewel-like precision,
entering every vital space, fading away,
traceless, o'er the rim of the world;

sea tones infuse feminine resonance,
sensual pleromatic, filtered through silk-like veils;
sonorous desires linger, echoes equivocate,
entranced and absorbed by opaline fog;

solar radiance envelops flowers, embraces the unseen;
crystalline spirals pulsate and caress each ear;
evanescent blooms of fire, whirling mellifluous *tremuli*
wherein translucent-winged dragonflies dream;

The Fine Structure Constant

serene mists soothe hard-edged *recontres,*
suffuse and soften raw-faced *naiveté;*
tidepools ebb, flow and condense; liquid cantatas bathe
and enter the air - the pure fragrant breath of the lotus;

nature's fugue does not atone nor demean,
it is not this, and it is not that;
melodic/metapsychic touch synergizes
a meaningful edifice of equanimity;

cosmic euphonies disperse throughout galactic ramparts,
and return to the source;
primal sound self-replicates - a shell
that intonates the universe in its own locution.

Sound is the hum of time-space contemplating the cosmos.

Projective (Revolutionary) Dimensions of Barbara Carlson's Art on Her Birthday

Who can say whether the asymptotic
alignment of her psyche and the stars
triggered the stirrings of mythical
artistic renderings.

Nevertheless, symbols surfaced beginning
as abstract leaf-like forms, still not
definitive, but hinting at hidden meaning.

Images developed further, and glimpses of
person-alities emerged, still not understood
clearly at absolute face-value.

The metaphor switched then to masks that
drew deeply from the group-soul
of the collective unconscious, and began
to show archetypal understanding.

Magic burst forth, to become Goddess
re-presentations telling truly who and

The Fine Structure Constant

what we were, and imploring us to
re-member the lost music and mirth-madness
of the great then, now and no-when.

Yet, what will come next? How will
further insight manifest itself on her
canvas? On this anniversary of her birth,
perhaps the mystery of the birth/death/re-birth
process itself will engender a new form of
seminal/semiotic communication.

All we can say (sense?) for sure, is
that novel creativity will continue; that
the infinite-eternal processual flux will find its
way into her art; and, most certainly of all,
the best is definitely yet to come!

IV.

The Search For Meaning

Point(s) of View

Thoughts trace an endless arc
in search of meaning.

Chaos offers up both truth and
mind-stripped entropy.

Order allows for precision, and
sterility.

The root, trunk, limb, stem and leaf
glisten ... speckled, yellow-green,
light-soaked ... yet trapped in
iridescent, scintillating, deliquescent
reservoirs of context.

Creation and denouement merge,
and disperse by way of
exegetic critique.

The Fine Structure Constant

The wind both listens and erodes.

Light is manifold, multiplex
and crystalline ... while at the same time
divisive, duplicitous and fractural.

The center both fuses and disperses
visions, visually ...
the edge reflects and absorbs intrinsic light,
reflexively.

Perspective and interpretation ...
light and dark ...
re-sounding vibrations ...
the wing-beat and spirit-flux of creative words.

Point(s) of view ... etc.

From Food-Chain to Mind-Link

One could, at times, almost believe
in a benevolent creator ...
if it weren't for the astonishing fact
that not only does our world meet all of the criteria necessary
for the construction of an elegant and classical laboratory experiment;
it further adds insult to injury by throwing all creatures (us included) into
a chain whereby we exist as food for each other's sustenance!

Of course it might be argued that ...
Homo sapiens, being at the top of the food chain,
is not eaten by others ... well, if not eaten physically,
then surely eaten psychologically ...
which in truth appears to be an even more terrible fate.

Original sin, karma, Lila/sport play, Christ as saviour,
the Tao, and/or the perennial philosophy (take your pick) ...
all have appeal, particularly to those with need of a belief system.
But, in view of the evidence, none of these 'systems' holds up
to solid critical/experiential analyses.

Of course it might be argued that ...
there is meaning in the cycle and process of humanity,
and that we simply can't understand or appreciate the divine master plan ...
well, rats in a maze might not sense the import of their significance in the

The Fine Structure Constant

larger scheme of things either (they only know of their plight).
Thus, by extension, do intelligent and critical humans interpret the existing
and overwhelming evidence which emphasizes their plight;
our angst and suffering are real,
(we are food and pawns in someone else's mindless game).

Descartes, Kant, Pascal, Buber ... (pick your intellectual mentor) ...
all employed exquisite reasoning in their search for meaning,
up until the eleventh hour, that is, when each capitulated by way of
'the clear light of reason', 'the things in themselves - not beholden to the
human intellect', 'the fearful sphere' and 'the I-Thou'.
It seems that without a 'God' hypothesis ... which is no hypothesis ...
but only the wishful thinking of a tired mind ... we must deal seriously
with a version of the Kant (without the cop-out) LaPlace hypothesis.

A rational and intelligent being would thus argue that ...
we seem to be thrown into a cosmos which, while exhibiting some signs
of elegance, meaning and intelligent reasoning, is nonetheless and for the most
part (to the extent that we ... now ... can determine) largely an animalistic,
insensitive zoo comprised wholly of boorish omnivores.

If there is truth and meaning in (our) contemporary life ...
it seems that it is only to be discovered
by dint of reasoning and compassion.
Nihilism, in and as practice, adds nothing to the equation;
but then neither does a non-explainable,
non-experiential 'spiritual' metaphysics.

Some might argue, though, that ...
it all might depend upon us ... that is, it might be up to us
to create the creation we *sense* to be enlightened.
Thus it would appear that we must find ways,

Keith Whittingslow

for all creatures,
to rise above the mindless, mechanical, self-consuming
food-chain.

The *way* might well be re-cognized (to know once again)
the omnipotence of the mind-link.

For starters, then, we might ...
Avoid premature closure (of mind), particularly with regard to theories
dealing with spiritual/metaphysical issues.
(Pyrrho's method employing suspension of judgment, with respect to
the larger
philosophical/theological issues continues to be peerless.)
Avoid category error, structure stage confusion, the pre-trans fallacy,
and legitimacy versus authenticity distortion; all of which are variations of
philosophical ignorance.
And last but not least, the avoidance of that which is least understood,
in civil and developmental terms, but deadly (and endemic in
our society) ... sleep deprivation.

The final argument (human denouement?) might then come down
to a choice between two mind-sets (two versions? two dreams?):
one which continues to employ a techno-logical, mechanistic,
self-ingesting, cyborgian view;
and the other, which would understand and deploy a mental arabesque,
with meaning, mind and the logos enscrolled moebius-like,
within that which is only mnemonically hinted, camouflaged,
and seemingly invisible ... universal mind.

The Fine Structure Constant

Food-Chain

⇕

Mind-Link

Here, at the edge of meaning and matter,
we direly need to extend our psychic senses,
and learn to see and know the pristine crystalline
filaments of truth that are everywhere evident to knowing seers.

Truth and meaning may well lie dormant, buried in our memories;
but they may also be readily recoverable by way of intellectually interpreted,
and interpolated ... *mind-linked* ... intuition.

The Interface

Between matrix and interstice -
essence.

Between concept and quality -
interpretation.

Between polar relativity and particular relevance -
perspective.

Between self and world -
idea/representation.

Between speech and logos -
thought.

Between matter and light -
energy.

Between universe and multiverse -
the akash.

Between body and soul -
the human central nervous system.

The Fine Structure Constant

Between speculation and contemplation -
intuition.

Between being and non-being -
the fine structure constant.

Between being and being -
I and Thou.

Between I and Thou -
the dialogical principle.

Between memory and the absolute -
truth.

Between image and substance -
meaning.

Between the conscious and the unconscious -
purpose.

Between process and reality -
imagination.

Between authenticity and means -
will.

The interface itself -
universal mind ... the abyss.

Origin

During intrajacent soul-ar ecliptic intervals -
the specter
of sentiently limned impressions
à clef
induces being's essence
from which
inchoate chiaroscuric forms
emanate -
to further swell aureolly.

The gnostic thrust
engenders morphic adumbrations -
- implicit facades -
which transmogrify explicate
essential images
spontaneously exuding
qualeae
at once both coruscative
and
transubstantial.

The Fine Structure Constant

From within
dream-like movements dislodge
primal intuitive fragments
and the soul
reawakens to consciously
recall ancient archetypal memories
of itself, and its origin.

Desire once again
permeates the stuff of life
dis-covering and projecting
pristine, ever-novel,
ontic and ontologic
(though ultimately provisional)
existential transpersonalities.

Meaning

True meaning -
is the *eidetic existent* (representational thought)
expressed in symbolic (sign) format.

By far
the best signs
are words.

Words
are best signified
and crystallized
as *belles-lettres*.

Language,
especially in its highest form - poetry,
shapes reality.

Reality engenders language.

Language engenders reality.

All of life (reality),
is an attempt to regain wholeness.

The Fine Structure Constant

Wholeness is meaning.

Meaning is wholeness.

Language … and interpretation,
bridge words, reality,
and meaning.

Humanity is myopic;
society reads the tabloids,
and is enmeshed in the now.

Meaning is atemporal;
it is always, and forever.

To know (and to understand) meaning,
we must escape time.

Poetry is atemporal.

Poetry engenders meaning.

Tears

Bittersweet *photismos* -
soul's fluvial plasma;
expressions of
profound joy, and
devastating sadness.

Spiritual purity,
hinc illae lacrimae,
compelled inexorably to transude
the obscure cataractic philter -
humankind.

Microcosmic spheres of crystalloid serum
brim o'er psyches threshold;
tensionally suspended droplets -
ontic quantae -
salient *essentiae* returning home
to the sidereal aether.

Tears are gifts;
agents of revision and transcendence,

The Fine Structure Constant

liberating, reconciling and evoking
atonement.

Tears
soften by compunction
the self-formed hardness
of the human
heart.

Trace and Texture

Signal *tractatus,*
glimmer of sign - vestige of truth;
equivocal *discernmente* -
impressions, mark, line, path -
symbolic miragical/image.

Aspectival *traversement;*
attributal qualiae - subtle character*i*stic;
psyche's engram,
limned representation.

Substantive textus - essential structure;
subtextual content -
metatextual weave; contextual composition;
cosmic warp - telluridic woof.

Hypertextual nanopointal superburst -
thermonucleotidinal (gaseous) fire-globes -
multiversal expansion;
elemental trace.

Macrotextual surface (textural) warmth,
star-sun, processual system(atic)
plant/moon condensate;
mind/matter substrate.

The Fine Structure Constant

Microtextual negentropic distillate -
enzymous blood-enfolded skin,
paraviscous, toroidally respired, globule;
breath-froth transudate.

Surface to surface,
surface to air,
air to air -
transrational metanoia.

Nexic, seamless, intermeshed
phase-linked sublimate;
transtextual metatrace.

Pantextual combinatory permutational hinge;
self-conscious individuation -
subliminal soul -
spirit.

Texture and trace.

Precision

With precision the heavenly orbs
transit their eternal paths.
Inexorably they are flung;
endlessly they track insensitive,
mindless tautological routes.
Their journey seems immutable, cold,
unconscious and fixed. They long
to know their fate, but they cannot -
they are condemned to chase empty,
chimera-embedded horizons.

All souls die all deaths.
Stars, mountains, trees - all labyrinthine
systems - including the demiurge, and the son
of man - die forever, their own particular,
recurrent, form of death.

Fate proffers hope and renewal;
butterflies, cetaceae, sequoias and humans -
all track their novel order.
Hope sustains, renewal intrigues -
penultimately.

The Fine Structure Constant

The *causa finalis* remains, eternally - storm and stress.

Each life form re-enters the fray -
transits the many poles - sways to the song -
is initially seduced, yet comes to know again the painful
rack of being's track - glory's illusion is in reality the *krystall nacht*.

The poet pierces all depths and unveils all shadows,
yet silently and longingly weeps.
He is alone - the single one, ever searching for truth -
eager to view luminous revelations - yet realizing being's lament;
all things seemingly transform - save the poet who foregoes the lure -
for one truth he knows precise - heaven too, is one more illusion,
one more device.

Analogues

Analogy is a relation of likeness
between two things, or of one thing
to or with another, consisting in the
resemblance not of the
things themselves, but of two or more
attributes, circumstances or effects.

A form of inference reasons that
if two (or more) things agree
with one another, in one or more respects,
they will (probably) agree in yet other respects.

Humanity, it seems, can only presently describe
itself, or any other thing, by way of
comparison and relationship.

Thus, something is
like
something else.

Metaphor, simile, sign, and symbol ...
thus point to analogues, and not to the
essence, reality, actuality or ...
the thing in itself.

The Fine Structure Constant

Everything is a counterpoint not only to
something else,
but also to itself.
Our attempts to define ourselves (and the other)
continue to be over against ... the other.

If reality (enduring spirit) is in fact
lit from within,
then we who peer darkly through earthly mist,
are indeed, poor seers of the akashic radiance.

We are analogous to that of which we know
and understand practically nothing;
we aspire to become anagogic.

As for myself, though I operate tenuously as a novice
dichter ...
and I strive to become a practicing anagoge,
I remain, for now, for better or worse,
an analogue.

Eidos

How are we to know that which is seen?
What is its form and shape -
to what is it akin?

Let us see.

Ether is a medium postulated
in the undulatory theory of light
as permeating all space,
and as transmitting transverse waves.

A cycloid is a curve traced by a point on a circle
rolling in a plane along a line in the plane.

Aer - (Greek) or mist (or air) is an invisible,
odorless, and tasteless mixture of gases
which surround the Earth.

Air in motion is any light breeze; hence breath, or breathing.

A fugue (from Latin - shining, fleeing, light)
describes a polyphonic composition
developed from a given theme,
according to strict contrapuntal rules.

The Fine Structure Constant

A musical canon is a composition of two or more voice parts,
employing *imitation* in its strictest form.

In biology, a cycle is a series of changes regarded as leading
back to its starting point.

The Greek atmo- is a combining form
meaning steam or vapor, and when
joined with the Greek sphaira (sphere),
becomes atmosphere - the whole mass of air
surrounding any celestial body or,
an encircling and/or pervading influence or,
the aesthetic tone or mood of,
or harmony of effects in, a work of art.

The Sanskrit atman - breath, self; is the life
principle, soul, or individual essence;
the universal ego whence all individual selves arise.

The Greek *eidos* is that which is seen;
an *eidolon* is an image, a phantom.

How then are we to see, to know, to aspire?

Quaerendo invenietis!

Tension

The eternal push and pull,
each cycle stretching
into a new dimension, sustains
emergent, gradient tensions.

Analogous, are fragments whose
singularities recall the whole,
and individuated agents
seeking continuity.

Space rebreathes time immemorially.

Where is the thread?
What is its purpose.

The tree of life
extends both above
and below the firmament;
suspended in a dream,
projected in thought,
yet reaching out, resolute
in the turn toward light.

The Fine Structure Constant

By design the thrust is committed to radical,
experimental, and random recombination.

The collective imposes tension
upon its composite parts,
and the parts seemingly unfold;
emanations and manifestations
of the all appear as no longer one.

It is what pervades both physical
and metaphysical systems -
the field's investment in being.

Lucid droplets, infused within
the oceanic colloid, reflect quasi-
spectralized and inconsequential distillate.

At a certain stage, metamorphoses evince
novel hierarchies - unseen, prior to
tensional realization.

The mystery diffuses, as a
conscious heuristic transudes
all realms.

The universal mind expands,
and quantum tensionally
converts knowing, simultaneously,
into both known, and knower.

Means to Truth

I

Castalia

A spring on Parnassus,
sacred to Apollo and the muses;
hence, source of poetic
inspiration.

A province of the spirit.

Any human institution devoted wholly
and exclusively to affairs
of the mind.

II

Das Glasperlenspiel

The Glass Bead Game;
one of a number of thought games
providing access to, and through,
the thousand-gated cathedral of
the mind.

The Fine Structure Constant

A symbol of human imagination.
A mental synthesis through which
truth and spiritual values of all ages
are perceived as simultaneously present
and vitally alive.

III

Willful Mind

Expanded consciousness bridges the gulf
between imagination and reality.
Conscious will contracts the interval of time
between first thoughts and final thoughts.
Where imagination culminates, truth is.
Eternity is always now.

Art and Science

How do we know them -
how do we practice them?

Living systems -
or theoretical constructs?

Art and science are at once
elements of human
perception and projection.

Both are invaluable as
social and cultural
heuristics, and
value systems.

Art amplifies the qualitative
and distinctive essence,
which is
characteristic of human experience.

Science contributes conceptual
parameters,
and interpretive frames.

The Fine Structure Constant

Wisdom, with respect to life's panoply,
is achieved
by way of the inclusion
of both
theory and praxis;
and their subsequent
synoptic union.

Art without science is blind;
science without art is empty.

Art and science are
dynamic equilibriants;
essential constituents
required for self/world
equanimity.

As universal ideas, and as particular
actions,
artistic and scientific
modes, *qua* life,
require great human proficiency.

Mnemonics

And so shall Jupiter's fiery fjords resound
with alpha and omega;
transliminal projections beam from then to now,
and back again.

And so shall inter-galactic star-spray evanesce
throughout light's immense journey,
permeating . . . reverberating,
invoking universal longing.

And so shall particulate mitochondria pulse
together with meteoric swell,
conjoining silence and source.

And so shall radiant multi-hued metachords reflect
deep-structured pathways,
embedded throughout, and within,
eternity's unified field.

The Fine Structure Constant

And so shall creatures once more explore
creation's moebioid frescoes,
as Genesis recants -
unfolding and evolving ever anew.

And so shall the dual-hemisphered human mind recall
the bi-polar fount;
multi-polar memory gleams, gracefully
renewing omniversal relativity.

And so shall the Logos remember
its purpose;
lucent images refracting
crystalline brilliance;
in esse veritas.

Still Life

I

Still life, as in art, as the subject in a picture consisting of inanimate objects, for example - fruit. Also the picture having this kind of subject. Already, for philosophers, subject-object difficulties begin to arise. A well known case - Cezanne; yet despite certain obvious agreements with respect to viewing, etc., Cezanne neither in his painting, nor in his commentary cares to offer any explanation or interpretation with regard to the *meaning* of still life depictions. By extension we are reminded of Beckett's refusal to explain or interpret the goings on in his play 'Waiting for Godot'. Artistic and poetic license, notwithstanding, 'Godot' the play (compared to a bowl of fruit) at least implies the existence of certain aspects of universal contemplation vis-à-vis eternal human questions of ontology, psychology and reality.

II

Still life, as in a place in space where star forces and planetary forces meet. Theoretically, at least, this stillness (was Ferlinghetti thus prescient in his use of *stilly?*) happens where particles stop their dancing spin and hang motionless in deep space. This is a *plasma*pause, a place of seeming equilibrium, yet subject to ongoing scientific *and* philosophical reinterpretation/redefinition.

III

Best of all, we have the poetic adverb *still*. Meaning always; ever; continually - to this, or that time; at present; *yet,* as words still used; in the future, as now and before; after that; after what is stated; as, 'he *still* feared'; ever more; even yet; as, *still* better; as conjunction - nevertheless, yet. This *stillness* of life, to me, addresses meaning head-on. It says that whatever rationale, with respect to art, physics, and/or philosophy we employ, there is always a remainder, an unknown. Yet it appears now as a part of the issue, and not as a separate non-referent. Somehow, I don't mind when the ineffable is an openly admitted referent and is included in the representation, thus taking on dynamic and fluid aspects of both theory and praxis. (Are art and science seen by their observers and practitioners as open-ended theories, or as self-encapsulated statements?) I would prefer the Cezannes, the Becketts, and the Stephen Jay Goulds of this world to flesh out their works with open discussion as to what their collective creative enterprises might, or might not mean. We may not expect absolute (*apodictic* as per Kant) definitions - but art and science without interpretation and critique only serve to further confuse many already poorly understood ideas.

IV

Still ... and yet ...

Primals

Allow fission's hues of garnet, verdigris and *kyanos,* throughout stellar realms, to *symbiose* with serum's binary blooms.

Allow the uroboric serpent, intrinsically lit and fusion-linked, to traverse inter-plasmic mind-brain loci.

Allow bird-song *tremuli*, floating codex, in endless movements, to echo *(rechercher)* from chromosomal oak to galactic rampart.

Allow Orion's sword to point our way, starward, past fiery globes, and planetary detritus, toward and back through Omega's reflexive telos.

The Fine Structure Constant

Allow the paw of the Manticore (with claws withdrawn) to tramp the Earth's span;   DNA limned teeth, triplex formed - *forsooth*.

Allow this scribe to breath, stretch, roam, and *leben dazeit* - in Physis' rhyme - both in real and imagined primal *sein*.

Eiron

Dissemblers In Speech

I

Paradox

Contrary to received opinion. An assertion or sentiment seemingly contradictory, or opposed to common sense, but that yet may be true in fact.

II

Either or?
Good or Evil?

Kierkegaard's thought, enroute to the single one, necessarily encompassed *both* good *and* evil. It is noted, though, that his version of existentialism is almost completely opposite the existentialism of the post-phenomenological/presuppositionless thinkers. Thus the single one recognizes (evolves toward) and becomes the whole one. How can an evil will exist, when God exists? The abyss which is opened by this question stretches into the darkness of the divine mystery. 'Unite my heart to fear thy name', Psalm 86, 11; ' ... for fear is the gateway to love' (Buber).

III

Irony

Simulation of ignorance. A type of humor, ridicule, or light sarcasm, the intended implication of which is the opposite of the literal sense of the words. A state of affairs, or a result opposite to, and as if in mockery of, the appropriate result; as, the *irony* of fate.

Socratic irony.

IV

Wit

Cognate to irony.
Activity of mind.

The power to evoke laughter by remarks showing swift perception, especially of the incongruous, and verbal felicity.

Wit-wita-witan (As.)
Intellectual power; sense, conceiving, reasoning, judging. Literally, wise men; to know or to have knowledge of; to learn; to be or become aware (of).

V

Too

A vessel whose content comprises fifty percent liquid, is *both* half empty *and* half full.

The Fine Structure Constant

VI

Satire
Cognate to wit.

Satura - a poetic medley; a dish filled with various fruit (possibly apples). Satiric (if not outright Satanic) verses.

~~~~~~~

Paradox, multiplicity, irony, wit, satire, sarcasm;

Dissemblers in speech.

Eiron

Etcetera, etcetera.

Syzygy

Archetypal images visibly appeared and limned the parametric potential of the *mysterium coniunctionis*.

Previously disjunctive projections reached critical mass, engendering (via morphic resonance) formative-causational morphogenetic fields.

Ontogeny recapitulated phylogeny; microcosm and macrocosm individuated; budding psyches freshly glimpsed telos and eschaton.

Thought and expression contemplated *aseity*; the divine Logos supra-liminally cathected, enabling more richly plangent utterances to resound.

Hermes and Aphrodite, for the first time, achieved lucent, transjunctive, interpretive (hermeneutic and hermaphroditic)

The Fine Structure Constant

consciousness;   Dionysus knew again pure paradisiacal godliness.

First and last things recognized their eternal and (at times hidden) unified fields; psychic anatomy (now soul-realized) - flourished, shining forth - web and matrix gleaming.

The Cosmic Self rejoiced in knowing anew, its own centeredness.

Stable, harmonious and balanced, syzygy rested - (briefly); then primal (repeto-cyclical) urges took hold, and *gnosis,* being inherently restless, began yet another journey - the perpetual hunt for its many-parted, chthonic-dwelling, heliotropic para-syzygouselves.

Synchronicity

Open Systems and Polar Dynamics

Synchronicity: an evolutionary dynamic, that is perhaps constant, but more often a hidden (thus paradoxical) variable. A correspondence between the microcosm and the macrocosm, directed through the personal psyche by way of the complexes. Connecting events that are independent of the cause and effect syndrome of linear time. Meaningful coincidences bridging different dimensions of time and space, aligning the prepersonal and transpersonal, with the personal, or the nonhistorical with the historical, and encompassing both matter and spirit. The delineation of a dynamic playing across the paradigmatic dimensions and energy fields of consciousness. A theory supported empirically by Sheldrake's explication of critical mass/morphic resonance and the formative causation of morphogenetic fields. A route to self/Self knowledge engendered by archetypal energy in concert with all of the many spectrums of consciousness.

The Fine Structure Constant

Open Systems: contravene the second law of thermodynamics and entropy; posit *dissipative structures* that allow for the birth of new forms out of chaos; recognize the influx of *new energy* in an open universe, and make room for the expectation of transformation.

Polar dynamics: although microcosmic personality supports the continuity of ego and self, it is nevertheless non-dual. At the level of the transpersonal consciousness, the polarity between microcosm and macrocosm, ego and self, masculinity and femininity, is monistic, not dualistic.

~

Thus archetypal fragmentation does not lead to polytheistic fragmentation, but to *androgynous monotheism*, or to the monistic self. Superconsciousness (the transpersonal unconscious) explicates conjunctionality and posits *both*, as opposed to *either or*, and resolves present-day consensual (contextual/category erroneous) conundrums.

~~

Consciousness, thus, is not an epiphenomenon of the brain; (although the brain *is* the seat of the actualization and translation of the archetypes in human affairs, it *reflects* the psychoid nature of the archetypes - their physical as well as their psychical imprint). Consciousness is *a priori*, and the brain is its instrument.

Seance

The littoral ambiance beckons -
benthic essence floods the air.

Sea sounds and scents; gulls, waves,
wing-beat, brine and kelp.

A certain coolness soaks the senses,
evoking a clarity of mind, and soothing
the frayed synapses of the soul.

One is lead (almost) to believe again;
but ever-recurrent thought,
obsessive, and relentless, forestalls
prolonged repose.

Never still, and always only partially present,
myriad multiverses enfold
before the seawashed, clear-bright, spunconscious
searching eye.

Transliminal exegeses appear, play out,
and vanish - only to reappear,
freshly formatted - begging (re)mindful attention.

The Fine Structure Constant

Endless visions, and versions of the cosmic drama,
seize the mind,
yet wash
and refresh psyche's center.

Deeply felt urges suffuse one's being;
primordial tides surge inexorably
nourishing desire - drowning numena.

The somatic séance scrolls on;
diurnal pulse ebbs and floods;
salient (daimonic) images swell inexpiably
from seas darkest depths
to lucent oceanic pleroma -
and back again.

Evolutes and Hermeneutes

The time is nigh for a surge - a shift - a bootstrapping, of particulate quanta and qualia, in order to reform the essential matrix of an exigent, revised, conscious understanding of eternal knowledge - and absolute truth.

We are evolutes of an unknown (and erring) force.

We are (to varying degrees) hermeneutes of these very deities, and forces.

All creation stories are myths to be reconceptualized in light of transmythic (transbiblical/transtextual) insight.

Consciousness evolves.

Popular testaments were, and are, based on an eager, powerful, but lesser and mistaken creator. Hence the paradox and confusion evinced from all legitimate theodicycal and ontotheological critiques.

The Fine Structure Constant

All classical good versus evil dilemmas (Abel/Cain, Abraham/Isaac, Job/Satan, Same/Other, You/Me) demand thorough reinterpretations - of and by both creator, and those created.

We have now, refined knowledge of physics/metaphysics, advanced (Jungian/Transpersonal) psychology, and more refined cognitive exegeses.

The intertestamental Gnostics were, it seems, ahead of their time.

Disparate dynamics, particularly those of Pistis/Sophia (Faith versus Knowledge) have yet to be fully played out. But, the evidence is mounting; archetypal complementarity, matriarchal/patriarchal splits, matter/spirit differentiation, and transtextual insights, are all in need of recontextualization - not to eliminate any of their aspects, but to reintegrate them with fuller authenticity and meaning.

All previously misunderstood dogmas are subject to refinement, resolution and wholeness. Transcendent, subtle, psychological syntheses imply a transbiblical/transtextual hermeneutic and ideology, in which the personal mode of existence finds a transcendence beyond its own transcendence of nature, a transformation beyond biblical redemption, a teleological future beyond the biblical future.

Transbiblical theology opens egoic existence to a radical re-rooting in a larger totality, a re-connection with the archetypal feminine, and a radical re-centering of human personality beyond the centeredness of the ego.

In the teleological age of transpersonal being, the microcosmic personality becomes the measure of all things, because in the microcosm the macrocosm finds at last its own centeredness.

The time is nigh for a surge - a shift - a bootstrapping, of particulate quanta and qualia, in order to reform the essential matrix of an exigent, revised, conscious understanding of eternal knowledge - and absolute truth.

Consciousness evolves (but requires initiative, self-actuali-zation, and constant reinterpretation).

We are (latent) conscious evolutes and hermeneutes.

Knowledge supersedes faith and leads to the pleromatic horizon.

Chalcedony

I

Agate

Late autumnal skies
of variegated chalcedony -
silvery chiaroscuric pastels -
vaulted (cloud-like) condensate -
cloaked (burnished/solar) amulets -
etheric (ruby) talismans -
pearly fissures limning the mind's cybernet -
being's plasma/CPU *qua* mind-set -
at once indigo-infused and super-suffused.

II

Verdure

Labyrinthine channels wend gloomily
throughout the mossy matrix of envy;
schizoid souls acquiesce to a pantheon
of duplicitous gods;
green-eyed fractals seemingly dance,
but actually tremble, with thoughts
of death - and worse, mortal condemnation.

III

Cerulean

Supernal azurean clarity dawns,
and lights a way to heaven.
Memory re-discovers, intuitively,
all truths - good, bad and indifferent.
Universal process is seen in transparent blue-gray hues,
like the mind's eye seeing itself, as well as,
the totality of all things.

IV

Chrysos

The golden breeze embraces primeval meadows,
enticing green chrysales of microid life-forms
to emerge from their lengthy gestations.
Dark, carnelian (chthonic) essences are transformed
into bright, eager, chromo-kinetic force-fields.
Desire vibrates and pulsates.
Kismet (destiny) is fully engaged.

~~~~~~~

The Fine Structure Constant

The web expands - infinitely satisfied,
yet ultimately (ironically) and fatally,
engulfs even its *self*.

~~~~~~~

Sentient life, overwhelmed, suffocates,
and shrivels to nothingness.

V

Kyanos

Aeons pass - another epoch begins;
blue-gold-green chalcydonic energy
crystallizes once again;
brilliance reflects and resounds
throughout space-time-relativity;
re-learning and reification,
of the eternal riddles ensue.

To wit, to know - means to pay homage
to the greater self.

Spinal Tap

The essential axis - the central spine -
the elastomeric fibrinous mesh encompassing
the ever-extending, evolutional, reach of being.

Oceanic thought-stuff, a salient web-like
colloid of body and soul; a sea of relationships,
in which, seemingly, we are immersed.
Human instinct, initially, is to harness that tide
(in order to influence and control it).
The realization, instead, is that we are captivated,
soaked in, and ultimately controlled by,
the sensuality of our own subjective gaze.

Nonetheless, object and subject have (paradoxically)
always been fused, and jointly, (yet strangely),
somehow, transmute each other in the act,
(and unlimited order of magnitude) of knowing.
We are, inexorably, the sum and compass
of our dynamic and reflexive vision.

The Fine Structure Constant

The mind's fluidity, in actuality, represents
nothing less than an infinitely extended series
of nodal plexae, which by virtue of their holding
dominion over the entire cosmos, are simultaneously
in both the present and the future.

This macro-noetic extension enfolds, at once -
evil, existentialism, and enlightenment -
and constitutes the immense constellational, and centrifugal,
surging, open-ended, willful/thoughtful (and eternal) unfoldment.

Synaptic conductants are manifold, and include
(but are not limited to) a primordial plasma,
a somato-psychic serum, a sentient universal
soul-star solvent, which together catalytically
engender the measureless amplitude of
elemental, rhythmic, energic mentation.

The next phase-dimensional emergence requires
a synthesis of alpha and omega (matter and mind),
and will be the culmination - the epochal movement -
whereby humanity taps fully and finally into the primal
sourceal qualia, the supernal noosystem of the cosmos.

As we plumb the depths of all things,
we will come to realize that there is no static center -
but an ever-flowing (cerebrospinaloid) fluvial axis -

Keith Whittingslow

which besides embodying the growing tip of evolution,
also baptizes, nourishes, and enculturates
a refined, unending, convergent, androgyno-conscious unity.

Helix

Thoughts spiral -
the spiral blossoms.

In the garden of ideas
I pluck the petals and leaves
of delirious silence.

Unspoken words imply
a flowering volute,
a living whorl
of twisted runes -
absorbed by twilight
(which represents the opening
glimpsed betwixt cosmic realms).

Memory's gyre recasts
slowly, yet inexorably,
the wasted embers of desire,
as well as an imperceptible spark -
the emergence of new form.

The vortex melds all images,
like flowing liquid,
a lucid dream, a reservoir,

Keith Whittingslow

a refractive essence,
like light ... lingual echoes
whose dancing shadows whisper
and describe meaningful geometries.

All being is conjectural.
All conjecture is helical.
All worlds are illusions.
All so-called realities are visions -
figments and fictions.

We exist on an incurved, horizenless,
Moebius wave, which scrolls forever,
in and throughout circles within spheres,
wound around celestial spiral corollae.

We travel the path of the heart,
and we are simultaneously
the traveller and the path -
the infinite empyrean helix.

Mica and The Pure Look

Martin B. saw it in a certain light
caught by a stone.

Edmund H. attempted to describe it,
(the process - the sense), as
a function of "The Pure Look".

What is experienced (Martin B. said "tasted"),
is unity;
Edmund H. would refer to the noemata,
the "phenomenological things in themselves".

They/It cannot be adequately described.

To talk around the issue is to talk of:
the disappearance of the distinction
between subject and object;
the elimination of the ordinary
relationship of polarity;
the transformation of the undifferentiated
state of the initial look (which is mere material),
to one of tensional form, which thus becomes associated;
the ordinary I, then, is a launching pad, a transformer,
a syntactical fact;
while the tensional I is a semantical *oeuvre* and a suchness.

Keith Whittingslow

So it is that we can talk about an internal flame,
and an undifferentiated unification;
we can talk about a phenomenological realm
of that which is being - and which pervades the matrix,
the interstitae, the core, the mantle, and the totality.

We can talk about direction, sense, polarity, archetypal and
metacosmic forms of unity, aspects of self and world,
and reality

We can, at present, talk of these things,
processes, shifts, transitions, experiences;
but as yet - to only talk, is to miss the mark of the exercise.

Perhaps someday (at the omega point),
we shall learn to talk of, and be - in actuality -
both the subjective essence (mica), and the
objective (pure look) of tensional sense -
simultaneously.

Mind Sutra

Hovering here on the fine edge of inter-atomic space-time,
juxtaposed amid mind and matter, we ponder
the human nervous system - the direct interface
between the physical realms as we presently understand them,
and the metaphysical realms envisioned in our thought experiments.

*Verticillary ramifications and nervural lineaments branch endlessly,
their ever-extending synaptic transducers and cyberneuronal matrices nourished
by the same sidereal plasma which bore primal-universal genesis.*

Teilhard envisioned, analagously, Ariadne's thread - the evolution
of the human nervous system - as both the directional thrust,
and the line of progress for life. Indeed, he posited deep psychic evolution,
the flowering of consciousness, as both the selective mechanism engendering
and supporting being's movement towards fulfillment, and the refutational
hole card attenuating science's tendency to postulate cosmic chaos.

*Thought occurs, and develops; consciousness proliferates throughout
many dimensions - from geogenesis (geotectonics, geochemistry, geobiology)
to biogenesis, onward to psychogenesis, and thence to noogenesis.*

The purpose, thrust, and meaning of evolution, then, is the generation
of self-reflexive conscious thought - thought which continues to expand beyond itself -
and the discovery of our *raison d'etre* and potentialities;

the mind is thus the overarching modality - the evolutionary *sine qua non* -
the exigent, expedient which is necessary for evolution's continual transformation.

The without, must, at the critical juncture,
fold back on itself and recognize the within;
the entire enterprise is one of perspective,
an enhanced, projective, engagement of the totality;
the whole of life is thus an attempt to see -
from within the framework of phenomenon and appearance -
the fullness of being which must be nothing less
than ultimate unity.

If life is, properly, at the forefront of scientific inquiry,
with all of physics subordinate to it,
then the heart of life, explaining its progression,
is the impetus of a rise of consciousness.

Seemingly our pace, in the ongoing process, is quickening,
as we transit the long evolutionary stretch - enroute to and through
the neuroontological psychozoic era;
we now glimpse, still dimly - but with increasing clarity -
the complex magnitude and splendor of the pleroma.

The mind is thus a double crystal -
both the essence and center of the self and of the world -
and the seer/knower of the great mystery *per se*.
It is not an accident that the word roots of both *science*
and *consciousness* derive from Latin (scire) meaning to *know;*
the thread that sutures all things together,

The Fine Structure Constant

is the light that reverberates between the reflections of the jewel of consciousness, and its own mirrored, infinitely inflorescent projections.

Logoic Enigmata

Seemingly language is a potion
  of the soma, the lingua, and the *thanata;*

the immense, sightless journey along
  the sword's edge, and within the flora
    deep in benthic canyons;

the hilarity that flouts convention
  and sacerdotal edicts;

the free-fall of drifting oratory
  into the abyss of parchment;

the angst that rides on diaphanous wings
  and traverses interminably the fearful
    dimensions of dreams;

the consanguineous simulation, the tragic defeat
  and ultimate *denouement* of the soul;

the truncated epiphanies,
  the occluded visions;

The Fine Structure Constant

the recognition of alter egos, rudely emerged,
   proliferating from recursive communal chinese boxes;

the tremolos on mnemonic ramparts and the
   chthonic shadows in mind's dungeon;

the evolution of thought, perspective, interpretation,
   endeavor and projection;

the florid syntax, thorny and ramified, embedded
   in the transgressions of writing;

the consciousness undetected, hence, unexpressed:
   hope against hope.

Semantic synapses.

Interlude

Momentary edifices
suspended in time;
semblant images, equipoised,
seemingly fixed in space -
ecce - transitional (translucent) spectrums
(framed - and unframed), flourish.

Resonant asymptotes emerge
and segue enroute to the inner and the outer;
reflective dianoic particles
encircle (and embrace) ratio's prism -
while constellational lattices (actualized quanta)
appear, but evanesce, mirage-like, into the void.

Plasma-limned verticils weave amongst,
and perennially enhance, the interstice;
as ideational formats - they conceptually endure,
yet as visual foci they vanish - similitudes of truth:

The Fine Structure Constant

spirit respires - in cloud's chamber -
I am the instant, as gnomon's pulse.

On the surface of the soul,
gravity reverses its charge;
thus life expands and contracts,
here and now, there and then.
Iridescent moments. I traverse
the event-horizon, in flux, for all of time.

Vectors

Something carries us along -
a force, a need, a longing for sodality;
a yearning for union.

A choice? A desire? A call?
A passion unfulfilled.
An urge deep within;
a quest - heart-felt,
yet incorporeal.

Beyond all living and dying -
a movement toward a richer place;
a sweeter domain, a more blissful realm.

The sinews stretch,
and the mind strains - now thrown,
now drawn, by tacit attractors.
Our souls must embark - but where,
and when? By what means,
measure, or gauge?

The heart's trajectory extends
in flight - through despair and pain ...
yet onward, transfixed - it aspires to sate

The Fine Structure Constant

a drive; to new dimensions? - or to
ab initio source? Perhaps both - to
a zone of knowing, at once transrational and
transcognitive - unthought of in
human dominion.

Spurred on by the unknown,
a whisper, a memory, a solar echo;
somatic ecstasy is convulsive voracity -
heart's embers need more - evanescence,
consummation - light filled tumescence
brimming pleroma's sum.

The Elysian Fields are not of physical matter;
neither are spirit's vectors born of desire.
One's being breathes only
through compassion,
one's essence radiates solely
from eternal fire.

Everything subsists in the contemplative breath,
(for now, uncomprehended, and seemingly uninspired);
a moving field (both *force* and *matrix*),
as yet unperceived, and thus unrequired.

Steady State

To assume a universe as having average properties
which are constant in space and time so that new matter
must be continuously and spontaneously created to maintain
average densities as the universe expands ... is likely, a partial view.

Present human vision distorts ... whether assessing self or *allos* -
what is seen, as framed by fixed referents and accurate parameters
- is relative.

There is a constancy, of a sort, but reality is not definable paragonally -
rather it (an inconstant constancy) is closer to being both parabolic
and paralactic.

The flux, visually, is *glissandic*, which is to say that events transpire
both within certain sets, and at the same time unbounded by any set,
or sets.

The human mind - is a net, or set, bounded (only) by its own
perspectival, and thus perceptual, limitations.

Friedrich N., was close to the mark in saying that
"there are no facts ... only interpretations".

The Fine Structure Constant

Systole is diastole,
and diastole is systole.

Didymos informed us that the source - *Quelle* -
is the exact opposite of our present understanding.

Didymos' twin advised that "he who seeks, continue seeking
until he finds. When he finds, he will become troubled.
When he becomes troubled, he will be astonished
and he will rule over the all".

Heaven and earth *are* rolled up in our presence ...
but one must find the hidden keys of knowledge (gnosis),
if one is to understand.

There *is* an image of the absolute reflected in the matrix of nature -
but it cannot be seen through an earthly lens.

There *is* a heavenly kingdom spread out upon the earth ...
but it remains unseen by earthlings.

What we seek - is already apparent - but it is unmanifest to the faithful.

The Fine Structure Constant - (a form of) a metaphysical steady state -

is knowable not through physics, nor chemistry, but only through psychics, and alchemists - that is to say through a radical, noetic readjustment of one's philosophy.

To know - we must think and search -
rather than believe and pray.

Ricercar.

Trope/*h*

Explosion

It begins ... (again) ... the primal (synechdochical) vortical ember
explodes ... particulate, spark-like photons download
omnichromatically and omnitemporally, fall into matter, and become
increasingly,
(structurally and phenomenologically) dialectical in their embodiment,
and in their polar antitheses.

Expansion

Chaotic turbulence, (always latent and cyclically patent),
emerges as inchoate meaning - conceptually foreshadowing
the eternal, immutable perfection of the divine circle,
which has neither beginning nor end.

Evolution

Vibrant intertextual vortices swell into gyres and double gyres;
intuition grows into thought - heuristic cognates become philoversified;
a corpus of waves develop through interplay and interaction into
polyvalent synchrony;
circularity, having achieved maximum dimensionality is transformed
into the universal

paradigmatic *torus* (which is thought to be the source, the holosystem,
all that is -
and of which all else are but subsets, minor representational variations
of the totality).

Involution

Ordered concatenation somehow exceeds helical tolerance;
what was once hidden (embedded) - and which subsequently realized
glorious manifestation - now recognizes the centripetal urge
to return to the center; nature is only penultimately canonical.

Contraction

Dis-covery leads inexorably to mobius reversal - a trochoidally
re-spired spirality;
becoming, at its zenith, recognizes the truth - that decay is inherent in
all component things -
- temporality must come full circle, to become once more - intemporal.

Implosion

It ends ... (again) ... the summation (the outbound/evolutionary and the
inbound/involutionary synthesis) flourishes, indeed magnificently, but
momentarily
at the omega point, only to enter into an immediate phase of deterioration,
random entropy and dissipation - recision - *deflourescence;*

The Fine Structure Constant

the hermeneutic circle - potentially symbolic of the most essential characteristic
of life (and poetry) hence meaning, ultimately collapses upon itself;
the foundation cannot hold; formulaically the process *Energy = Gravity*
once more reabsorbs its muse (itself) - hope implodes, a victim of its own machinations -
the experiment enfolds, rolled-up into silence - extirpation, emptiness,
the still-point - awaiting primality *redux,* which after repose and aeonic rest,
breathes new light-sparks into play, turning the singular(total)ity, paradoxically,
back into the omniplurality;
thus the trope/*h* emerges, grows, achieves fullness in time and space -
know itself to be the
complete expression of spirit (while understanding the exigency of all turns -
the eternal revolution within the flame of regeneration) -
ergo (de trop) - mind's reconvolution.

About the Author

Keith Whittingslow is an independent scholar whose passions are philosophy (particularly philosophy of mind), poetry, and interdisciplinary consciousness studies. He lives in northern California with his wife Pat, and a magical cat named M.C. (Molte Colore).